STOIC
AT
WORK

This book is dedicated to my mother, Elizabeth Lawson,
a former corporate high-flyer with no filter and no tolerance
for anyone boring or with body odour; and to David Lawson,
my late British father, who was also a business owner
and introduced me at a young age to the most comically
dysfunctional workplaces in the TV shows *Blackadder*,
Fawlty Towers and *Dad's Army*.

STOIC AT WORK

~~50~~ 49 MODERN RULES

Ancient wisdom to make your job a bit less annoying

ANNIE LAWSON

with illustrations by **Oslo Davis**

murdoch books
Sydney | London

CONTENTS

'At dawn, when you have trouble getting out of bed, tell yourself: "I have to go to work – as a human being ... I'm going to do what I was born for ... or is this what I was created for? To huddle under the blankets and stay warm?"'

Marcus Aurelius, Meditations, *5.1*

INTRODUCTION

It is Tuesday. The worst day of the week. Nothing good happens on a Tuesday. You look at your diary and see that your day is filled with back-to-back meetings. Even so, you have a board paper due, a training module on ethics and compliance to complete, and Rhonda from procurement keeps calling about a spreadsheet.

The only thing keeping you going is the prospect of after-work drinks later in the week, where everyone shares their horror stories from the front lines. Over several glasses of wine, you slide into existential despair at the realisation that you have no choice but to work for your entire life. Until you die.

Some people resent having to give up their creative dreams and earn a living. They are angry at the amount of time their job consumes, and at how it dictates what they wear, when they eat lunch and whether or not they can take a holiday. And at being forced to do it all again, day after day. Those who feel they have landed their dream job complain that it does not come with a dream salary, so they must persevere until robots are developed that can take over their function.

The problem is lack of choice. Rather than steering the ship of our own lives, we are deckhands slaving away to keep someone else's enterprise afloat. The conveyor belt of work is enough to dampen anyone's spirit.

Besides, the whole apparatus of work is not designed to make us happy. It is designed to reward us for our time and skill. If anything, the system is indifferent to our moods. Otherwise, it would not entail so much frustration and drudgery.

'There are people at work that I wouldn't save from a burning car,' one colleague tells me. 'I'd rather be dead than go back tomorrow.'

Things are no better among my school parent group. One has broken her knee in a work-related injury yet is still required to dial into work meetings. Another says she is working just to fund her stash of Band-Aids to cover up her blisters from wearing heels into the office. A friend who works as an emergency nurse was fed up with being yelled at by ice addicts. I'm working to replenish my lost mobile phone cables, which seem to disappear as often as socks.

The only person I have heard recently who actually loves their job is the character Death from the Neil Gaiman book turned Netflix show *The Sandman*. 'Lots of people don't have a job they love doing, so I think I'm really lucky,' she says.

The trouble with working is that you're obliged to front up with a go-getting, can-do attitude every single day. And for many of us work is bookended by a commute. That means your days start and end with you standing uncomfortably close to someone on the train who has a runny nose and no tissue, or is eating a squelchy banana, or is having a loud but non-critical phone conversation about whether to have chicken or pasta for dinner. Or you're stuck in traffic, clocking up a mountainous fuel bill and suppressing the urge to rage at people who drive one-handed with their forearm dangling out the window.

Once you make it into work, you listen to other people type, chew and breathe while you attempt to get some work done. You fritter away money on a soggy schnitzel sandwich and a few takeaway coffees. When you're forced to 'hot-desk', your exposure to bugs dramatically increases. And the carousel of meetings with no outcomes eats away at your soul.

By the time you get home again, the pantry is empty, the clothing pile is Himalayan and the house looks as though it has been ransacked. You collapse, brain-fried, on the couch, with a glass of alcohol in one hand and your phone in the other, and spend the next few hours scrolling brainlessly to dull the pain.

The carousel of meetings with no outcomes eats away at your soul.

Deskless jobs in education, health, construction or emergency services that are critical to the functioning of society also have their frustrations. Friends in these jobs make those of us who complain about office politics look like superficial whingepots, given the life-changing situations they are confronted with daily. Yet people in these jobs must also contend with annoying people, defective bosses, unsustainable workloads and meetings with no purpose.

It has always been easy to find things about our jobs that we dislike. The danger in identifying shortcomings in our circumstances is that it's much easier to blame work than ourselves. If I step in cat poo, it's work that has made me feel tired and disorientated. If I cannot open the lid on the peanut butter jar, I blame work because I have not had time to lift weights. If someone cuts me off in traffic, I curse the driver's employer for distracting them with work worries.

But, as with everything, there are some upsides to working. Indeed, work life can sometimes be fun. My workmates and I often compile the worst phrases we've heard in meetings recently, such as 'move the needle', 'deep dive', 'step change' and the dreaded 'reach out'. 'Today has been a real paradigm shift,' one colleague said, before realising in horror he had become just another corporate hack.

A sense of community in the workplace can also help break the monotony. Work can even become a place of seismic change, where your job actually contributes positively to the planet. But mostly work is just a stage for mild irritations. It is also complex, filled with power struggles, tensions, competing priorities and a whole bunch of Rumsfeldian unknown unknowns. Which makes the downsides much more fun to complain about.

My scientific method for finding ways to cushion the blunt force of relentless work was to consult colleagues over wine and beer and brainstorm some techniques to survive the sheer frustrations we all feel. That inspired me to start writing a genuine self-help guide to tackle the realities of working alongside a random collection of people you would not normally cross the street for.

But I needed more.

Some years ago, I was in a meeting to discuss an event at which the CEO would deliver the keynote speech. He wanted to go big and discuss global problems and opportunities in order the 'shift the dial'. A project plan was discussed, timelines agreed upon and responsibilities assigned.

Then it was on to the next meeting, in a different room but with the same décor – beige walls, all modern artwork and swivel chairs – and, as it turned out, the same people. We smiled at the coincidence. The discussion was about another event in which a C-suite executive planned to give a keynote speech about challenges and opportunities of a global nature in order to 'move the needle'. Another project plan was pulled together, deadlines made and roles handed out to those in the room. We finished six minutes early because we knew the drill. 'That's six minutes back in your diaries,' the project manager triumphantly declared.

I checked my diary, and there was another meeting just before lunch. I joked about seeing the same crew in a few minutes. Turns out they were in the next one too. We decided it was pointless

— 5 —

moving meeting rooms again. Then someone said we needed to 'innovate' our approach and 'reimagine' our meeting processes, whatever that meant.

This triggered existential angst in me about whether work was just about talking to the same people about the same things, day after day. A revolving door of meetings until we all fell off this mortal twig.

'Are you okay?' the project manager asked.

I was not. 'Is this it?' I asked her. 'A lifetime of boring meetings with no purpose and mind-numbingly repetitive conversations about events that don't matter in the grand scheme of things?'

There are certain givens in the land of work, the most immutable – and career-limiting if ignored – being not to complain to a workplace snitch. Which I just did.

At lunchtime, I went to a bookstore down the road and scanned the self-help and philosophy sections for some inspiration. Wedged between *Dealing with People You Can't Stand* and *100 Tricks to Make You Appear Smarter in Meetings* was a copy of *Meditations*, the self-help bible written by Roman emperor and Stoic philosopher Marcus Aurelius. If business heavyweights like Bill Gates and Warren Buffett, not to mention actor Arnold Schwarzenegger as well, had faith in the power of Stoicism, it was worth giving it a go.

The ancient Stoics knew a lot about hardship, warfare, disease, toxic people and death, which makes them more than qualified to offer guidance on the travails of working life.

I soon realised that *Meditations* is essentially a practical guide for managing stressful situations and difficulties, and therefore perfect for navigating the politics and tribulations of the modern workplace. The ancient Stoics knew a lot about hardship, warfare, disease, toxic people and death, which makes them more than qualified to offer guidance on the travails of working life.

Stoic philosophy was founded in Greece by Zeno, a wealthy and successful merchant who was shipwrecked on a trading voyage and nearly lost everything around 304 BCE. His life changed when he was introduced to philosophy by the Cynic philosopher Crates of Thebes, who was heir to a large fortune but renounced this for a life of poverty on the streets of Athens. Building on the moral ideas of the Cynics, Zeno founded Stoicism, a philosophy that advocated a life of virtue and harmony with nature as the best means of achieving peace of mind. 'I made a prosperous voyage when I suffered shipwreck,' Zeno said.

Marcus Aurelius Antoninus (121–180 CE) embraced Stoicism as an operating framework for managing his job as Roman emperor, one of the most powerful positions in the world. Although Marcus is regarded as the last of the five 'good emperors', his reign was marked not only by military conflicts, a plague and health troubles, but by plenty of annoying people too.

He was not the only notable Stoic philosopher. Playwright and political adviser and mentor to Roman emperor Nero, Lucius Annaeus Seneca (c. 4 BCE–65 CE) invoked the wisdom of Stoicism in *Letters from a Stoic*. Seneca's ambitions were curtailed by a lung condition, forcing him to take time out in Egypt, where he wrote, read and recovered. In 41 CE, a decade after Seneca had returned to Rome, the emperor Claudius exiled him to the island of Corsica, where he began his discipline of letter writing to console others and himself. Seneca felt sorry for anyone who had been spared misfortune. 'You have passed through life without an opponent,' he wrote. 'No one can ever know what you are capable of, not even you.'

The Stoic philosopher Epictetus was born into slavery around 55 CE, and faced many difficulties. His violent and depraved master snapped Epictetus's leg and left the young man with a permanent limp, an injury he viewed as an impediment only to his leg, not his character. He was eventually freed and later founded a philosophy school in Greece. Epictetus became an influential philosopher whose insights are captured in his *Discourses*.

These three Stoic heavyweights embodied the four virtues of Stoicism: courage, temperance, justice and wisdom. The world of work is inescapably riddled with challenges that the four virtues can help us face, if we can integrate them into our daily habits.

The single most important practice in Stoic philosophy is differentiating between what we can change and what we cannot. Epictetus famously said that our 'chief task in life' is to identify what is outside of our control – and that, he pointed out, is everything other than our own thoughts, choices and actions. These alone are within our control, so they are all we need to take responsibility for.

And this, it was clear to me, is the perfect mindset to bring to the modern world of work.

Time spent worrying about things we cannot actually change is pointless.

A colleague sits next to you breathing like Darth Vader? Move desks. You wish you'd become an astronaut rather an accountant? Do something space-related as a hobby. Your boss gives you an hour to pull together a PowerPoint presentation? Manage their expectations by setting out clearly what you can realistically do in that timeframe. Time spent worrying about things we cannot actually change is pointless.

It's easy to be overwhelmed by whatever challenge is confronting us on any given day. Seneca advised to prepare for difficult times even when you're feeling secure. We should 'balance life's books each day', he said, and prepare our minds as though we are already at the end of our lives.

Adopting Stoic thinking is a good way to handle the ups and downs of any working life. When we suffer setbacks, Marcus advised: 'Do not suppose you are hurt, and your complaint ceases. Cease your complaint, and you are not hurt.' Moreover, obstacles are really learning opportunities. 'The impediment to action advances action,' he said. 'What stands in the way becomes the way.' A meeting that goes nowhere is a lesson in patience. A hostile colleague is a lesson in fortitude.

Stoic philosophy provides a general perspective on the work universe, existential consolation for those times when work sucks, and practical advice on making the whole experience much better and more fulfilling.

Marcus's insights into managing tricky people are just as relevant today as in the second century CE. So too his perspective on incomprehensible corporate guff and the political scheming that all leaders must confront. He came to expect that people would be frustrating, and knew that taking a measured approach was the best way for him to stay on top of his game and not let his work take over his life. 'Be not heavy in business, nor disturbed in conversation, nor rambling in your thoughts,' Marcus said. 'You must always preserve in yourself the virtues of freedom, of sincerity, sobriety, and good nature.'

When I read those lines while flipping through *Meditations* in that bookstore, I realised he was onto something.

That afternoon, in an all-divisions meeting of 50 people, our team leader asked for someone to volunteer a 'safety share' (see Rule 7). The room fell silent and everyone looked at the floor. Safety advice usually constitutes things like 'make sure you hold onto the rail when walking down the stairs', 'don't trip over any equipment' or 'don't eat someone else's lunch'. But it felt a bit awkward because we didn't work in a place where safety was critical.

Eventually, I stuck my hand up and suggested everyone start the day by using insect repellent. Why was this necessary unless you worked outdoors, someone asked. Because, I said, then you won't get a flesh-eating bug that mosquitos carry around, that might cause you to have all your limbs amputated. The leader gave me a look – *Are you bonkers?* – and moved on to the next item of business.

It was only a mildly humiliating moment. But why, I asked myself, should I let it bother me at all? The Stoic approach would be not to worry about what other people think, given their thoughts are outside our control. If I applied the Stoic virtues more broadly, I began to see, I could perhaps make work a place of joy, or at the very least a bit more tolerable. Maybe I could become indifferent to other people's opinions of me, more patient in meetings that dragged on, more forgiving when a vendor was abrasive, more courageous when things inevitably fell apart and the workplace descended into a *Lord of the Flies* situation.

The following rules apply the ancient wisdom of Marcus Aurelius to the frustrations of the modern world of work – from annoying people and incomprehensible jargon to meetings with no outcomes and co-workers who eat pretzels on the loo. Some of the Stoic quotes in this book have been tweaked for clarity, though occasionally archaic words such as 'thine' and 'thyself' remain. (While I advise against using them in the workplace, they are preferable to contemporary abominations people use to describe themselves like 'dynamic symbiotic engagement facilitator' and 'strategic thought leader'.)

RULE 1

ACCEPT THAT PEOPLE
ARE ANNOYING

People are, for the most part, annoying. And disappointing. They have been since the dawn of humans.

Annoying people are everywhere. Colleagues, bosses, subordinates, CEOs, CFOs. People who work in legal and procurement, in classrooms, on worksites, in hospitals and in shops. And then there are those *The Economist* branded 'the consiglieri of the corporate world', management consultants, regarded by some as well-paid advisers and by others as exorbitantly charging salesman. Annoying people cut across all work categories and all industries.

When you click with your workmates, there is no greater joy. The banter is good, the work quality high and the after-work drinks entertaining. But when you do not, working life can become unbearable.

What makes them so annoying? Is it a desire for attention? Relentless ambition? Or a just a terrible personality? The latter may manifest as mild sniping, relentless backstabbing, unreasonable negative feedback, even outright office warfare.

Even worse are those annoying people with baby voices. Katie from customer support used her baby voice, with a pitch like the squeal of a tyre burnout, to tick off a friend of mine, Emily, for booking a weekly meeting with her at 12 pm on Wednesdays. Emily had barely hit send on the invite before Katie strode up to her desk, grim-faced.

'I note you have put in a recurring meeting each week at midday,' Katie squeaked. 'As leaders, it is really important we respect each other's personal time. In my team, we do not book any meetings between 11.30 am and 2.30 pm so people can eat lunch at their leisure and at a time of their own choosing.'

Emily said not much in return – because she felt homicidal. She later texted me: 'WTF!!! Between no early meetings, lunch and school pickups, I reckon these doopers work four hours a day. Tops!'

At a previous workplace, Sharon from finance took annoying to a whole new level. Her chief task appeared to be parroting whatever the boss said. If he said: 'I think we need better processes,' then Sharon would instruct his team to 'really think about developing better processes'.

Sharon was also in the office choir and felt it appropriate to use the medium of song to tell colleague Angela what to do. 'Angelaaaaaa,' she trilled in a soprano voice. 'I've got some more work for youuuuuu!'

Angela was juggling a heavy workload and her day was already out of control. And besides, Sharon was not her boss – she was just a nobody trying to become a somebody by delegating work. Angela wanted to the let the tide of annoyance wash right over her. Or, even better, to respond in kind: 'Sharonnnnn, could you please kindly shut the eff uuuuup!' But instead, she shot her a dagger look and silently vowed to have nothing more to do with her.

What do the Stoics say?

Marcus Aurelius was an analytical and creative thinker who liked to contemplate life's big questions in peace, without intrusion from others. If Sharon or Katie had walked up being 11/10 annoying while he was considering a matter of imperial significance – a battlefield perhaps, or the welfare of his people, or the political infighting of the day – he would pause before responding.

Should he find them irritating, as he no doubt would, he would first say to himself: *I myself have many faults and am no different from them.* Then he would ask whether he was even sure that they were doing wrong. Marcus would reflect on Katie's baby voice and Sharon's singing and ask: *Who am I to judge?* 'One must be thoroughly informed of a great many things before he can be rightly qualified to give judgement,' he wrote in *Meditations*.

He would step back and put the moment into perspective. 'When you are most angry and vexed, remember that human life lasts but a moment, and we shall all of us very quickly be laid in our graves,' he told himself.

Marcus started each day with the expectation that he would encounter angry, stressed, impatient, ungrateful people. 'Begin the morning by saying to yourself, I shall meet with the busybody, the ungrateful, arrogant, deceitful, envious, unsocial. All these things happen to them by reason of their ignorance of what is good and evil . . . I can neither be injured by any of them, for no one can fix on me what is ugly, nor can I be angry with my kinsman, nor hate him.' Preparing his mind in this way helped him control his responses better.

He also accepted that the world did not revolve around him. 'It is a great folly not to part with your own faults which is possible, but to try instead to escape from other people's faults, which is impossible,' Marcus wrote.

When you feel the temptation to launch a verbal grenade against a Sharon or Katie to prove a point, Marcus would say, don't match their tone. Instead, step back and listen. Silence is a more powerful response than desperately trying to prove a point. Anger undermines our ability to reason and empathise.

A measured response in the face of an annoying person takes the heat out of our reaction to them. Marcus reminds

RULE 1. ACCEPT THAT PEOPLE ARE ANNOYING

us: 'Rational creatures are designed for the advantage of each other . . . a social temper is that which human nature was principally intended for.'

Even so, it is worth noting that Marcus may have disposed of his own work colleague, the co-emperor Lucius Verus, in 169 CE. There were rumours Marcus had Lucius poisoned because he gambled and failed to take his responsibilities as co-emperor seriously. So perhaps even Marcus had days when he could not follow his own advice.

A FINAL WORD FROM MARCUS AURELIUS

'If anything external vexes you, take notice that it is not the thing which disturbs you, but your notion about it.'
Meditations, 8.47

RULE 2

ACCEPT THAT EVEN BOSSES CAN BE ANNOYING

A tricky peer or consultant is one thing. But a tricky leader can make or break a job.

Being downstream from someone at work gives you a true insight into their character. Are they relaxed and easygoing? Do they promote and acknowledge the efforts of their team? Or do they take credit for your work, knife their underlings behind their backs, launch grenades in meetings or have unsavoury habits?

The signs are there early for those blessed with acute observational skills. Is your boss a good timekeeper with meetings? Do they give you a pat on the back for a job well done and suggest areas of improvement and advancement? Or are they late without any apology? And when they arrive, do they sit there backstabbing your colleagues for their incompetence, but reassure you that 'you're okay'? If the latter, you could either start looking for another role in the organisation, or get a friend to call them and say you're incapacitated for as long as the job lasts.

I once had a boss who read me the riot act when I went to the bathroom and forgot to lock my computer. He said this was necessary to prevent the criminals who apparently roamed the office from stealing sensitive information from people in the loo. Even if the only sensitive information on my screen was a targeted advertisement for a tent dress. He was quick to anger if you didn't telepathically understand what he expected of you despite not briefing anyone, took the credit for anything good his subordinates did and looked like a cross between Homer Simpson and Jabba the Hut. If he was injured by a mob of emus, I wouldn't have lost sleep.

A friend had a boss who earned the nickname 'Itchy & Scratchy' because of his habit of scratching his groin. He stood over his team, who were seated, and continued scratching as he assigned them work.

Another had a boss who screamed at them centimetres from their face if she was ever displeased – which was often. One boss treated staff like primary school students, reading excerpts of the book *Who Moved My Cheese?* to them. This was the same leader who scrapped the employees' bonus scheme – a quarterly payment of 10 per cent of salary – and replaced it with the gift of a corporate-branded leather jacket with money stuffed in the pockets.

One ex-colleague said his boss referred to herself in the third person as 'Mumma'. She would say, 'Mumma will not be happy if she finds out any of you have applied for another job . . . Mumma will kill you.'

If you leave a job because of a shabby leader and start another job hoping this time things will be different, there are no guarantees it will be any better. You begin with a sense of optimism, but soon you realise your leader might be just a tad annoying. Your view of them darkens and maybe you refrain from confiding in anyone that the boss is a pain in the backside.

A deeply unreasonable boss can undermine your mental state and be potentially tedious if you go on about it to colleagues. Treat a highly dysfunctional boss as though they are vomit splatter on a footpath and get as far away as possible. But an annoying boss doesn't necessarily mean you have to jump ship. Finding common ground, setting boundaries and staying a step ahead just might dial down your frustrations.

What do the Stoics say?

Marcus Aurelius studied leaders he admired and found that the best ones developed their character, worked hard, embraced criticism, lived simply and did not crave praise. However, we should try not to allow ourselves to be troubled by difficulties upstream. The only things that 'affect the soul', Marcus said, are our 'internal beliefs'. He believed that there is no need for your mind to be rattled by people or outside events, unless you interpret them as being harmful.

Nobody is perfect, and the chances of a leader in the workplace being flawed are extremely high. But the problem is not them – the problem is how we react to them. The single most important practice in Stoic philosophy is differentiating between what we can control (and therefore change) and what we cannot. What we have influence over and what we do not.

If your boss barely speaks to you, causing you to conjure up frantic thoughts about how poorly they think of your work, they are probably just an introvert with a big workload. If they dump a heavy workload on you and sell it as a 'step-up opportunity' (see Rule 35), then it's time to control what you can and have a chat about expectations, no matter how unapproachable your boss may be.

Marcus ruled from 161 to 180 CE and built a reputation as a wise leader who aimed to be 'like the promontory against which the waves continually break, but it stands firm and tames the fury of the water around it'.

He believed that, as emperor, it was important for him to avoid the 'imperial stain'. 'Have a care you do not have too much of a Caesar in you, and that you are not dyed by that dye,' he wrote. 'Be candid, virtuous, sincere, and modestly grave. Let justice and piety have their share in your character; let your temper be remarkable for mildness and affection, and be always enterprising and vigorous in your business.'

RULE 2. ACCEPT THAT EVEN BOSSES CAN BE ANNOYING

Leaders must not assume a godlike aura, he believed, given they had the potential to falter just like everyone else. Good leaders were mindful of people's humanity, dignity and pride when making decisions, and avoided the trap of making quick judgements about the actions of others. They also controlled their emotions and calmly dealt with problems as they arose.

A FINAL WORD FROM MARCUS AURELIUS

'The gods live forever and yet they don't seem annoyed at having to put up with human beings and their behavior throughout eternity. And not only put up with but actively care for them.'
Meditations, 7.70

RULE 3

DON'T USE CORPORATE FLUBBER

L anguage emerged from chaos and has evolved, been reshaped and reformed across generations.

In the workplace – and in corporate workplaces especially – language evolved to become more nonsensical. Words are strung together in baffling sequences that often make no sense at all.

Normal language has been supplanted by some horrendous constructions – 'thought shower', 'unpack', 'value proposition', 'greater granularity', 'reach out'. The prefix 're-' is almost randomly added onto words – re-imagine, re-energise, re-align. Other phrases that are indispensable in the corporate workplace include 'move the needle', 'shift the dial', 'ideate ideas', 'circle back', 'deep dive' and 'wheelhouse of skills'.

George Orwell once said that 'good prose should be transparent, like a window pane'. In his view, writing should never draw attention to itself or obscure meaning. If we extend his analogy, corporate writing these days is like triple-glazed frosted glass.

Why say 'I'll take a look' when you could say 'let me sense-check that'? Instead of saying, 'Can you summarise that?', go for 'I'd like a high-level take on that'. Rather than 'I'm taking notes', you say, 'I'm holding the pen'. Sending out information becomes 'cascading the messaging'. Anything useful you have learned is 'a learning'.

The use of 'journey' outside the parameters of travel has infected workplaces. At a recent yoga class, the teacher welcomed us 'on our journey together'. At a restaurant, we ordered the chef's 'effortless journey' banquet. When a business goes pear-shaped, it's described as a 'challenging journey'.

The rules of grammar are routinely ignored. For instance, some writers in the business world like to use so-called zombie nouns – verbs dressed up as nouns – as it makes what they're saying sound more important or technical that it really is. This allows you to say 'We will provide you with the information sharing' when what you really mean is 'We will tell you something'.

Sometimes words can cost a company money. When things go horribly wrong, many leaders like to be ambiguous about who is responsible. 'An incident took place' is better than 'we had an incident' because it leaves ownership of the stuff-up open.

Using waffle appears to be a tactic aimed at impressing people with complex turns of phrases. Yet it can backfire because people might think you are concealing something. The investor Warren Buffett, whose shareholder letters are so succinctly written that they are considered the gold standard, calculated that people would be worth at least 50 per cent more if only they mastered the art of clear communication.

What do the Stoics say?

The Stoics valued clear, concise communication, including correct grammar, diverse vocabulary, smooth expression, succinctness and audience-appropriate messages.

Marcus Aurelius found clarity in the simplicity of doing your job. He would say that precision and brevity help you understand your goals and explain them to other people. They make it easier to identify what is important, so you can get things done more easily.

In a letter to Marcus Aurelius, the Roman rhetorician, grammarian and senator Marcus Cornelius Fronto praised the emperor for never using 'a far-fetched word' or 'unintelligible' figure of speech. 'A Caesar's eloquence should be like the clarion,' Fronto said.

Indeed, *Meditations* is written in clear and powerful language, reflecting Marcus's own respect for reason and judgement. He believed unhappiness and evil stemmed from ignorance and a lack of clear thought. Scan his self-help bible and you won't find any convoluted writing or odious phrases like 'cascade' or 'reach out'. A lack of clarity, he believed, led to a blockage in thought or actions.

But Marcus was not snarky about others. If someone said to him, 'Let me reach out to our internal best-practice team to connect with world-class capability,' he would not reply, 'WTF are you on about?' Rather, he would reflect on the person delivering the gobbledygook and try to decipher their motivation and the true meaning of what they were saying.

A FINAL WORD FROM MARCUS AURELIUS

'Do not dress your thought in much fine talk. Be short in speech and restrained in action.'
Meditations, 3.5

RULE 4

DON'T DELIBERATELY CONFUSE AUDIENCES

Before she retrained as a teacher, *Financial Times* columnist Lucy Kellaway waged a 25-year war against corporate guff. She concluded that 'business bullshit has got a million per cent more bullshitty'. The problem, she said, was that those who talked tosh were unbothered. If you bore your audience to death, they will never hold you to account.

This was the operating framework that Steve from partnerships felt could advance his career. Bamboozle your audience with incomprehensible twaddle and they will be too confused to challenge anything you say. Steve wore a blue checked shirt rolled up at the sleeves and dark trousers, and glided around the office, with a smile that was reserved only for senior leaders. It dropped for anyone below executive level. He was as slippery as an eel doused in oil, and loved adding the prefix 'geo' to words to sound smart. 'I think we need to geo-curate content that we geo-fence, and then geo-release it at the right cadence . . .' Sometimes his comments were so incomprehensible that it was hard to know how to respond.

Once, after I suggested an idea in a meeting, Steve responded with: 'Thanks – that's a really good point. But your contribution did not match the geostrategic objectives of the geo-curated narrative framework.'

At first I thought he was complimenting me, and I felt the warm glow of someone who has just been praised. Then I wondered if maybe he had imparted some great wisdom. Finally, it dawned on me – he had just decapitated my idea.

That's the beauty of this mystifying language, which is thoroughly widespread these days. In that office, anything anyone wrote was routinely subjected to the corporate blander. What began as a lovely piece of writing would come out the other end sounding like a pile of excrement.

Convincing bosses and colleagues to avoid jargon was an uphill battle, as one 'teams value proposition' drafted by a team leader made clear: 'We stretch our reputation by providing strategic leadership as custodians of our words that signal a paradigm shift to investing into understanding how we seek to influence our content management modules.'

It went on: 'We pull the outside world in and wire it to the internal business though informed, measured, considered and constructive advice that supports and nurtures leaders to ideate their ideas and make decisive decisions. We are clear thinkers who deliver solutions-focused outcomes and an investable proposition.'

The team's value proposition made it look like we were doing something, but really it just meant that no one actually knew what the hell we were supposed to do. Ultimately, there is no need to impress anyone with convoluted turns of phrases.

What do the Stoics say?

What if Steve told Marcus Aurelius that his 'contribution did not match the geostrategic objectives of the geo-curated narrative framework'?

Marcus would lean back in one of those vinyl meeting chairs that swivel around and ponder Steve's nonsensical words. He would conclude that we should not be bothered by other

RULE 4. DON'T DELIBERATELY CONFUSE AUDIENCES

people's actions. What they do is their problem, not ours. Our focus should be on discarding our own misperceptions about them.

Removing our judgements about others also removes the emotions of irritation, frustration and anger. Do not tether your mind to what other people say and how they say it. Marcus spoke about freeing yourself from the 'whirling chaos' that blows in from the outside to give the mind greater clarity. This frees the mind from the bombardment of jargon that clouds our understanding of what it is we're actually meant to do at work.

Speaking the truth, doing what's right and accepting fate means, Marcus said, that you should 'strive to live only what is really your life, that is, the present – then you will be able to pass that portion of life which remains until death, free from perturbations, nobly, and obedient to your own spirit'.

A FINAL WORD FROM MARCUS AURELIUS

'Always go by the shortest way to work. Now, the nearest road to your business is the road of nature. Let it be your constant method, then, to be sound in word and in deed, and by this means you need not grow fatigued, you need not quarrel, flourish, and dissemble like other people.' *Meditations*, 4.51

RULE 5

BE PREPARED FOR THINGS
TO GO OFF THE RAILS

The increasing shift to online meetings has exposed us all to more IT trouble than ever before. Especially for those of us not blessed with advanced IT skills.

There is a moment in most online meetings when everyone's on mute, except the host and some sucker who accidentally unmuted themselves while ticking off their partner for leaving the kitchen cupboard door open. The rest of us wait with great anticipation to see if the drama will escalate or if the sad soul will realise her error.

The host steps in. 'Lizzy, you're not muted . . .'

Lizzy frantically mutes herself, but it's too late. We all now know she is finnicky about kitchen cupboards, and we vow to tread carefully around her the next time we're in the kitchen at work together.

Presenting in an online meeting has its own challenges. Sharing your screen, in particular, can be a fraught exercise. Especially when the thinking icon takes too long and everyone in the meeting shakes their heads and says, in unison, 'Your screen isn't sharing.'

Then, as soon as the screen shares successfully, up flashes an unflattering email about Rhonda from procurement. The email, sent by her boss, says that Rhonda is unbearably annoying and spits when she speaks. We all wonder how he'll explain that one to Rhonda – and to HR, who will inevitably wade into the drama.

To break the ice, I unmute myself and start to explain the intricacies of reputational risk. Only, I have accidentally logged in twice, so my voice has an echo. All everyone can hear is me saying 'risk, risk, risk, risk'. The host steps in and asks me to 'take it offline'. At least he didn't ask me to 'circle back'.

I agree, then he continues: 'Do you mind circling back to the group with any key learnings?'

My key learning is to have nothing more to do with circle back man until the end of time.

What do the Stoics say?

The Stoics exercised a technique known as *praemeditatio malorum*, which means imagining the worst-case scenario in order to ensure you're not surprised by unexpected negative events. This is one of many psychological strategies Marcus Aurelius used to manage his emotions and his reaction to life's difficulties.

The dichotomy of control espoused by Epictetus helped Marcus endure obstacles that derailed his plans.

Epictetus said: 'The chief task in life is simply this: to identify and separate matters so that I can say clearly to myself which are externals not under my control, and which have to do with the choices I actually control. Where then do I look for good and evil? Not to uncontrollable externals, but within myself to the choices that are my own.'

Epictetus said that, actually, we humans control very little. We do not control what happens to us, or what people around us say or do – and we cannot fully control our bodies, which are susceptible to illness. The only thing that we can control is how we think and the judgements we make about things, people and events.

What is under our control is our own will. Things happen to us, but we are in charge of how we mentally respond to them.

Stoicism encourages us to take more ownership of our thoughts, our actions and our responses to situations.

There are times, of course, when things are beyond our control. When IT lets us down, we can take the Stoic approach and brush off the uncontrollable. Even better, if we anticipate an IT meltdown, we'll be pleasantly surprised on the odd occasion when things go smoothly.

A FINAL WORD FROM MARCUS AURELIUS

'One's own mind is a place most free from the crowd and noise in the world, if a man's thoughts are such as to ensure him perfect tranquillity within, and this tranquillity consists in the good ordering of the mind.'
Meditations, 4.3

RULE 6

THINK LESS

There is nothing more annoying than when people say 'Don't overthink this'. After all, everything requires thought. Who are they to judge whether your thoughts are overcooked?

And yet in the workplace, overthinking comes with the territory when there's been a monumental stuff-up. The kind of mishap that wakes you from a deep sleep at 3 am. Your mind goes into overdrive as you desperately search for ways to reverse time and make the mistake go away, even though you don't have the resources to fix anything. After a while, when the heat of fluffing a work project subsides, you mentally shunt it into the funny story repertoire and it consumes no more thought.

A friend, Susie, arranged a conference for educational leaders at which the principal of a training college was scheduled to give a keynote speech. At the event venue, a lectern, chairs and banner were set up, catering was ordered and audio-visual technology tested. It was only when the principal turned up and saw the conference centre was completely empty that Susie realised she'd forgotten to invite the educational leaders.

She agonised over the stuff-up. But to what end? None whatsoever, given she had no ability to change the outcome and make them magically appear at that moment. Excessive rumination did not reverse the mistake.

Other friends had similar horror stories. One hired a project manager who told a web of lies instead of doing any actual work, and derailed the whole enterprise. After the project manager was frog-marched from the building, an inspection of her locker revealed it was stuffed with important project documents scrunched up into balls.

The problem is not how to prevent stuff-ups from occurring, but how we recover from them. How do we move from blind panic to intense worry and then to negative reflection? The biggest problem is our belief that people will think worse of us after a failure, and that it might thwart our chances of career progression – or even result in us losing our job.

One way to stop the overthinking cycle is to be aware that you are doing just that. There is nothing solid or permanent in our thinking. Thoughts evaporate like clouds, to be replaced by new thoughts that are equally transient. Letting go of the idea that there is truth in these thoughts can be helpful. It takes the heat out of our mind, and can help us move on to taking action.

What do the Stoics say?

The Stoics paid close attention to their thoughts and feelings. If Marcus Aurelius had failed to invite educational leaders to an education conference, he would take a step back and separate his judgements and opinions from his attention and wisdom.

Marcus made plenty of mistakes during his time as emperor. Worse than forgetting to invite any guests to an education conference, he appointed as his co-emperor and eventual successor his son Commodus, who was manifestly not up to the job. Even the wisest rulers will slip up sometimes.

Overthinking is fuelled by anxiety. It denies and avoids the reality of the present moment: you're either worrying about past events, which you have no ability to change, or about things that haven't happened yet.

Marcus advised that we should 'consider how many men have embroiled themselves, and spent their days in disputes, suspicion, and animosities; and now they are dead, and burnt to ashes. Be quiet, then, and disturb yourself no more.'

He also paid attention to his thoughts and perceptions in order to better manage his concerns. 'Your intellect is not affected by the roughness or smoothness of the currents of sensation, if she will retire and take a view of her own privilege and power,' he noted.

A FINAL WORD FROM MARCUS AURELIUS

'You have it in your power to have no such opinion, and thus to keep your soul undisturbed. The external things themselves have no power of causing opinions in us.'
Meditations, 6.52

RULE 7

ABANDON IRRELEVANT
MEETINGS

There are two types of face-to-face meetings. The first type is productive, efficient and results in decisions and actions. Then there is the other type, in which a piece of your soul dies.

Another friend, Sarah, who works as a counsellor experienced the latter when she was summoned in person to a 50-minute meeting with her supervisor, Amanda, to discuss whether another meeting was necessary. Sarah had a busy day with back-to-back clients and resented Amanda adding pointless meetings to her crowded schedule.

'There was no outcome,' Sarah said. Meetings about meetings rarely end well.

Things were no better for a former workmate of mine, Barry. Ahead of his team meetings at a cycling retail business, everyone had to fill in a spreadsheet with what they intended to talk about, and this was circulated to the team. When they gathered for the actual meeting, everyone read out their spreadsheet entry without any further discussion. 'Utterly pointless time waster,' he said. This was after he attended another meeting, which had the title 'Financial Enabling Refresh Discussion'. The name was apparently the highlight.

As noted earlier, I've been to meetings that began with a 'safety share', where someone shares a lesson based on a personal experience to spare others the same mistake. That might be life-saving in genuinely hazardous professions, but for those of us who work in offices, the biggest danger is running out of ideas for the safety share. After a while we're talking about paper cuts and getting stuck in the elevator.

Some argue that high meeting loads sabotage productivity. But others say a well-run meeting constitutes meaningful work. Meetings with too many people at least allow you to disappear, so long as you nod occasionally when someone important speaks or promise to 'circle back' if someone asks you a question. The satirist C. Northcote Parkinson estimated that five people in a meeting were 'most likely to act with competence, secrecy and speed'. If this grew to nine people, two of the nine were 'merely ornamental'; at 21, 'the whole organism begins to perish'.

Unless you want to be an ornament, it is best to keep meetings small and the discussion focused. That way, you will be pleasantly surprised when you leave with a plan of action.

What do the Stoics say?

Sniping at colleagues in meetings is not, the Stoics would say, natural. The greatest contribution we can make is to be cooperative. Stoics use reason and logic to manage difficult situations.

Marcus Aurelius would not tell Amanda to shove it up her backside for arranging a meeting about meetings because he did not condone emotional outbursts or loss of composure. Do not let posturing, sniping or petty behaviours in meetings be a distraction.

As emperor, Marcus always attended the Senate's meetings when he was in Rome, often staying late into the night. As we have seen, he began his day with the expectation that he would meet with troublesome people. That way, he was not disappointed when his decisions were questioned, his time was wasted and his goodwill was exploited by others, and he mentally prepared himself to deal with such challenging behaviours. And if none of it happened, he was pleasantly surprised.

Marcus conceded that life itself was warfare. Humans are capable of awful things – like Barry being forced to fill in a pointless spreadsheet or Amanda booking pointless meetings in an already overcrowded schedule.

We are at our best, Marcus said, when we work collaboratively towards a greater cause, and help others. He advised a liberal dose of perspective, so we might remain calm and keep space clear for things that actually matter. To make meetings more productive, focus on creative problem solving, and change course when an obstacle appears. Encourage dissenting opinions in order to sharpen your thinking and produce a better result.

A FINAL WORD FROM MARCUS AURELIUS

'We are made for cooperation, like feet, like hands, like eyelids, like the rows of the upper and lower teeth. To act against one another then is contrary to nature; and it is acting against one another to be vexed and to turn away.'
Meditations, 2.1

RULE 8

BEWARE TECHNOLOGY IN MEETINGS

It was a Thursday morning when I looked at my diary and saw six online meetings booked for the day. First up was a risk and audit meeting. Next was a meeting about processes and opportunities with 11 people. Another with ten people followed, about overhauling a customer system. Meanwhile, Fiona from marketing slotted in another meeting straight after, titled 'Better ways for Annie and Fiona to work'.

Sitting for eight hours listening to pointless twaddle can lead to heart disease, type 2 diabetes, obesity and insanity. What better way to break up the tedium and frustration than combining your meetings with lifting weights or practising downward dog? Except that is a terrible idea. Because whenever you think the camera on your computer is off, it is most likely on.

If only the Canadian MP who appeared naked during a virtual parliamentary sitting in 2021 had realised this; he was getting changed in his office. He's not alone, of course, given how many online meetings Covid lockdowns forced on the business world. But to avoid embarrassment, just don't get changed during meetings. It can wait! Or even better – plan ahead so you're wearing the right outfit for the meeting, like you did back in the pre-pandemic days.

Also, just check if your camera is still on. Or put a sticker over the lens if you simply must overhaul your outfit.

Unfortunately, the managing director of one software company conducting an all staff and customer 'town hall' followed none of these rules. Instead, he thought it wise to change into a suit and tie as the meeting got underway. He exposed more than just his thoughts on the organisation's direction in what quickly became a viral video.

Similarly, if you think you're muted, you're probably not. Saying to a flatmate during a 12 pm meeting, 'I just need to show my face to these stupid people and then I'll join you for a surf' could be career-limiting if you haven't double-checked. It works both ways, too. If you think you're not muted and share your thoughts expansively on a project, chances are that you are muted and no one heard anything.

What do the Stoics say?

Work assaults us on every front with uncomfortable situations. Awkward banter in the office. Unhappy customers. Accidentally appearing butt-naked in online meetings. Had Marcus Aurelius lived in a time of Zoom meetings and disrobed without knowing the camera was on, he would not allow himself to succumb to humiliation. He would instead use perspective to diminish the sheer embarrassment of being tackle-out on the telly.

'How unfortunate has this accident made me?' he imagined someone asking. 'He should rather say, What a happy mortal I am for being unconcerned upon this occasion.' Elsewhere, he said: 'Here you must remember to proportion your concern to the weight and importance of each action. Thus, if you refrain from trifling, you may part with amusements without regret.'

The Stoics believed there is no need to act on your mental impulse unless you assent to what it tells you – which in this case is that you should feel humiliated.

'Your manners will depend very much upon the quality of what you frequently think on,' Marcus said. 'For the soul is as it were tinged with the colour and complexion of thought.'

Before you follow the urge to react to a difficult situation, take the time to consider your response. 'All things are opinion, and . . . it is your own power to think as you please.'

Marcus believed we have the choice to not turn such excruciating situations 'into something'. Being a better person throughout your life is more important than being fleetingly regarded as an idiot. Even a naked idiot. Some people might still think you're an idiot, despite your best efforts. If so, be respectful but disregard them in favour of truth and knowledge.

Besides, we'll all be dead soon enough, so best not to waste time worrying about accidentally flashing your colleagues.

A FINAL WORD FROM MARCUS AURELIUS
'If this accident is no fault of mine, nor a consequence of it; and besides, if the community is never the worse for it, why am I concerned?'
Meditations, 5.35

RULE 9

DO SOMETHING. ANYTHING

It is easy to wallow in inactivity when your inbox is overflowing, Nathan from IT keeps asking you to download a new version of Teams, and the CEO rings to tell you the report you slaved over was rubbish.

The pandemic turbocharged workloads for those who kept their jobs. The number of meetings exploded, project demands grew and work became a pressure cooker. People became more fractious. For me, the disorder at work spilled onto the home front. Dirty socks were left abandoned in the living room, a nest of snails moved into one of my sons' rooms, and giant lint balls rolled down the hallway like tumbleweeds. All this translated to a very cluttered brain.

When things seem overwhelming and insurmountable, the only thing to do is start small. You are better off doing something, anything, rather than sitting there worrying about it.

I could explain to my son that if he did not leave apple cores on the floor, then the snails might not have set up home next to his bed. Or I could throw the abandoned socks in the bin. Or ignore the planet-sized lint balls. Or accept the mess and just get on with my work.

Of course, it's easy to blame work for your lack of progress. Who wants to clean after a long, hard day in the office dousing spot fires and juggling deadlines? The mind conjures all sorts of justifications as to why something cannot be completed. But making a decision is an action, even though on its own it does not change anything. In these circumstances, doing something, anything, is all it takes to make progress. Consigning a task to some mythical future means it will never get done. And doing something imperfectly is better than dreaming about doing it perfectly.

British author Oliver Burkeman wrote in his book *Four Thousand Weeks* about the 'Pomodoro Technique', a productivity method devised by software developer and entrepreneur Francesco Cirillo in which you set a timer and work in 25-minute time blocks, breaking for five minutes in between each one, then taking a longer break. The ticking clock creates the illusion of an external deadline, and builds the self-discipline muscle. This mental trickery jolts the brain out of inertia, limiting daydreaming, mindless scrolling and other distractions.

Of course, some people have no respect for work boundaries and will contact you at all hours, regardless of how disciplined and efficient you are. These people are to be avoided if possible.

What do the Stoics say?

Stoicism offers some excellent advice about taking action, whether that be a decision to do something or not. Deferring action until some magical time in the future when everything is suddenly perfect is a road to nowhere. As Marcus Aurelius wrote: 'It is just that you should suffer, because you neglect your present business; and would rather become a good man tomorrow than today.'

He believed in giving full effort and attention to each action, in order to achieve the best outcome, and aimed to complete each task with as much diligence, enthusiasm and commitment as possible. As Marcus saw it, that is the right thing to do.

How does this apply to Patricia, a disgruntled checkout assistant in a supermarket who flings the groceries towards

the bag area? What about those days where everything goes wrong, your enthusiasm plummets along with your productivity, and you start resenting the path your life is on? Marcus would say that we can choose to do our tasks with a better disposition, and simply endure whatever comes our way. He said that 'everything harmonises with me which is harmonious to the universe'. This might then help us feel better about our circumstances when they feel less than ideal.

What should you do if you turn up in the morning and forget your password and lock your computer after three failed attempts at logging on? Or if HR demands that you complete three online courses about cyber safety, risk and processes before lunchtime? Instead of feeling paralysed by the task ahead, just start on some easy aspect of it so you feel you're making progress.

There will be days when other people's priorities hijack our working day, in which case our focus shifts to managing our reactions to these new demands. We can interpret this as unfairness and wonder what point there is in trying, or we can reframe the situation and see it as an opportunity to learn about endurance, patience, resilience, struggle.

And if you want to get something done, then the best thing is to start actually doing it.

A FINAL WORD FROM MARCUS AURELIUS

'Remember how often you have postponed minding your interest, and let slip those opportunities the gods have given you. It is now high time to consider what sort of world you are part of, and from what kind of governor of it you are descended.'
Meditations, 2.4

RULE 9. DO SOMETHING. ANYTHING

RULE 10

DO NOTHING

There is an alternative path. Do nothing.
This may seem counter to the previous rule of doing something. After all, Marcus Aurelius said that 'you can . . . commit injustice by doing nothing'. If there is something that needs doing but we avoid it because of the effort involved, it is laziness.

And yet former British prime minister Lord Melbourne coined the phrase 'masterful inactivity', while General Electric chairman and CEO Jack Welch scheduled 'looking out the window time'. Strategic idleness can enable you to gather your thoughts, sidestep drama and determine the right course of action.

There are many things in life that cannot be improved with greater effort. Sometimes it is better to take a step back. The law of reversed effort (coined by the author Aldous Huxley) says that the harder you try, the harder you fall. Trying too hard can be counterproductive. His advice was to step back from the action and let things unfold.

A former colleague of mine was also a big fan of doing nothing. He worked in corporate affairs and his job was to put out reputational spot fires before they grew into raging bushfires. But often, he said, they would put themselves out; sometimes intervention only provided additional fuel.

'The best thing I've learnt is to do nothing,' he said. 'It's brilliant advice but very difficult to actually achieve, as people either automatically panic or want to be seen as having a solution to difficult situations, thereby justifying their existence. It's incredible how often doing nothing turns out to be the exact right approach.'

As he saw it, doing nothing takes less effort, causes less angst and means that when you leave work for the day, you're in a better frame of mind. Not leaping to a decision also created the space for him to contemplate the issue in depth and ultimately make a more measured choice. 'Think about everything like a chess game,' he told me. 'That is, always try to think several moves ahead. The "do nothing" approach allows that to occur.'

His next piece of advice appeared contrary to the 'do nothing' argument, however, and was a deal more scatological. It's always a good idea to face up to a serious problem as soon as it occurs, he explained – although what he actually said was to 'eat shit sandwiches while they are warm, as there is nothing worse than a cold shit sandwich. And you don't want them to become the whole, à la carte smorgasbord of shit sandwiches.'

What do the Stoics say?

Sometimes, it is good to pause before you react. Wrap some space around an issue and let it marinate before moving into solution mode. That way, you can calmly focus on what action to take.

According to the Roman historian Cassius Dio, Marcus Aurelius would sometimes 'consume whole days over the minutest point, not thinking it right that the emperor should do anything hurriedly'.

When you feel a swell of emotion in response to an unpalatable situation, suggests Epictetus, you should first pause. Allow the heat of the situation to dissipate. This gives you time to consider your response, instead of allowing your emotions to control your thoughts.

Epictetus saw wisdom in taking such space. 'It is essential that we not respond impulsively . . . take a moment before reacting, and you will find it easier to maintain control'.

Instead of viewing situations through the filter of emotion, taking a step back and acknowledging and accepting the emotion from an external perspective creates space. If your colleague or boss makes you unhappy, maybe it is okay to be unhappy. This perspective can put a buffer around the unhappiness, and make the situation matter less.

But given Marcus viewed doing nothing as an injustice, then maybe do just a little bit of nothing, and later, when you have reflected on the situation, do a little bit of something.

A FINAL WORD FROM MARCUS AURELIUS

'In one way an arrow moves, in another way the mind. The mind indeed, both when it exercises caution and when it is employed about inquiry, moves straight onward not the less, and to its object.'
Meditations, 8.60

RULE 11

DON'T PROCRASTINATE

Of course, doing nothing can easily veer into the realm of procrastination.

Many years ago, I started writing a book called *Seven* about a character who went on a family trip to Italy and broke her arm in a town called Alberobello in Puglia. The town is renowned for its *trulli*, which are conical huts dating back several hundred years and adorned with magical symbols painted on the roofs. Anyway, my main character goes into one of these huts for medical treatment, and when she emerges an hour later she has lost seven years – and her family, who have moved on. It's basically the same premise as the show *Manifest*, in which more than five years elapse during a flight from Jamaica to New York, leaving the passengers to re-integrate into society with great difficulty.

Even though my book pre-dated the show by many years, I only got as far the title. A decade on, I had still written nothing. Instead, I used my spare time to imagine how incredibly successful the book might be. There would be advances, awards, speeches, maybe even a film. The possibilities for success were great. Yet the bar for success was so high that it was easier to do nothing.

The problem was distraction. Procrastination comes from poor self-regulation rather than poor time management. It is also bad for your health, because focusing on short-term comfort over long-term goals causes stress. It's unsurprising we dither as a deadline looms. The very word 'deadline' – a point in time by which something needs to be done – was originally a line drawn on the ground in prisons. Prisoners who crossed it were shot. No wonder they induce such dread.

Despite this, we still put things off until the pressure becomes so great that we find ourselves in a worse position, having created more stress as we frantically produce substandard work. Chronic procrastinators would rather improve their mood by avoiding work in the present than finish a task that has future benefit. Time slips through our fingers as we mindlessly scroll, post, tweet and email. And what have we got to show for it? Nothing.

There is a meme that neatly sums up the different types of procrastinators:

- **WICKETKEEPER** – puts on gloves and stands back
- **SENSOR LIGHT** – only works if someone walks past
- **NOODLES** – thinks all jobs take two minutes
- **BLISTER** – appears when the hard work is done
- **SHOWBAG** – full of shit
- **LANTERN** – not very bright and has to be carried
- **DECKCHAIR** – always folds under pressure
- **G-SPOT** – you can never find them
- **WHEELBARROW** – only works when they are pushed
- **CORDLESS** – charges all night but only works for two hours

There are days when the 'sensor light' approach to the working day seems a sensible one, because it's just easier to put things off when you're overwhelmed.

What do the Stoics say?

Marcus Aurelius advised himself to 'perform every action as though it were your last; if your appetites and passions do not cross upon your reason . . . and do not complain of your destiny'.

Time is a currency far scarcer and more valuable than money. You cannot get it back. And the worst time-waster of all is procrastination, according to Seneca in his book *On the Shortness of Life*.

'Putting things off is the biggest waste of life,' he wrote. 'Postponement . . . deprives [people] of each day as it comes, it snatches from them the present by promising something hereafter.' His conclusion was that the 'greatest obstacle to living is expectancy'.

It is hard to start something without the certainty of an immediate reward. The payoff might be hours, days, weeks, months away – or longer. Incentives that link a commitment to a reward – such as eating a piece of chocolate once you have done a certain amount of work – can help curtail short-term impulses. But it does require at least a smidgen of willpower to not reward yourself willy-nilly.

Seneca was not tolerant of those who squander time. He said that 'life is long enough, and a sufficiently generous amount has been given to us for the highest achievements if it were all well invested . . . So it is: we are not given a short life but we make it short, and we are not ill-supplied but wasteful of it . . . Life is long if you know how to use it.'

So how do we avoid procrastination? By identifying potential distractions and impediments that might derail our project ahead of time and avoiding them. And if your workplace has more than a few showbag, lantern and G-spot procrastinators, good luck.

A FINAL WORD FROM MARCUS AURELIUS

'Do what nature now requires. Set yourself in motion, and do not look about to see if anyone will observe it; nor yet expect Plato's Republic: but be content if the smallest thing goes on well, and consider such an event to be no small matter. For who can change men's opinions?'

Meditations, 9.29

RULE 12

CARE, BUT DON'T CARE

S ome years ago at a drinks event with colleagues, I asked those who had reached the top of the corporate tree for their insights into how they became successful. Some of the advice sounded like corporate blather: 'Be part of a journey to transform from good to great' and 'Make it work for you'. But others had some very useful insights. The main theme was to not care too much about what happens at work.

'Care but don't care' was the catchphrase of the night. But what exactly does that mean? Doesn't that leave you in a care vacuum, if you both care about something and don't care at all?

One former workmate elaborated. 'Everyone cares about work. It is impossible not to, as it is so bound up with our identities and our egos. But most people care too much,' they said. 'They get obsessed and caught up in issues that actually don't matter. Obviously, we all care about what we do. But we should just let some things go. Don't care too much.'

The trick is not to let niggles at work take up too much of your mental space. In the office, focus on the benefits – the freely available coffee (unless it is instant), the funny colleagues (if there are any) and the well-stocked stationery cupboards (unless someone else has already nicked the lot). At home, relish the upsides of minimal grooming and commuting, and the ability to churn out work from bed. Moderately care about things that go wrong without obsessively ruminating on them.

Some lucky people seem to breeze through work because nothing much bothers them. They are either sociopaths or the kind of people who can naturally swat away annoyances. They simply refuse to engage in the anxiety-inducing ups and downs of the workplace.

How can the rest of us care less about work?

What do the Stoics say?

A Stoic is not concerned with what others think. Their focus is on independent thought rather than blindly following the crowd.

Marcus Aurelius was conscientious about neither flattering others nor inviting praise. While it would be a stretch to say he was breezy, his writings suggest that he imposed limits on what he cared about. He cared about taking charge of his thoughts, focusing on what he could control, taking on board criticism and leading a simple life. He believed that wishing for a different reality was pointless when his efforts could be directed towards something more meaningful.

It is a waste of precious energy to be annoyed by people's shortcomings and things they say. 'I have often wondered how it comes to pass that everybody should love themselves the best, and yet value their neighbour's opinion about themselves more than their own,' he observed.

The universe is impartial to our struggles and our desire to bend reality. The collision between our perception and reality creates an illusion that fuels disappointment. Marcus suggests viewing a problem from telescopic perspective, so that we might understand its true significance.

A FINAL WORD FROM MARCUS AURELIUS

'The power of living well is seated in the soul; if it
be indifferent toward things which are indifferent.'
Meditations, 11.16

RULE 13

SUCK UP, BUT DON'T SUCK UP

Whether to suck up or not is a hotly debated subject in many workplaces. Most people roll their eyes at suck-ups, yet stroke the vanities of executives themselves at some point in their careers.

The suck-up hovers near the boss and other important people, delivering well-timed compliments. They mirror the boss in meetings with infuriating comments like, 'That's an excellent point and I've been thinking the same thing' and 'I couldn't agree more that [insert what the boss just said]'.

There is a continuum. At one end is paying a simple compliment to a senior leader, motivated by normal human decency and with no hidden agenda. At the other end of the spectrum, there is full-scale, vomit-inducing brown-nosing in order to get ahead; clearly, this is fuelled by ambition and ego.

Though it's excruciating to watch, the workplace rewards suck-ups. If you take a strong, principled 'no suck-up' stance, do not be surprised if your bootlicking colleagues leave footprints on your head as they climb up the greasy pole. More annoying than witnessing a suck-up is the realisation that it is effective.

Most careers have only a few defining moments: getting a first job, winning a promotion, maybe landing a big deal. The rest of the time we lurch from one mini-drama to the next, with nothing much of note in between. Being caught in the crossfire of a suck-up situation (SUS) qualifies as a mini-drama.

A rich source of SUSes is the 'diagonal slice', where workers are randomly selected to have lunch with senior leaders in an effort to bridge the hierarchical divide. In this scenario, your job is to listen to the leader talk about their success, ask a couple of follow-up questions and then slink back into obscurity. Unless, of course, you are a suck-up. Then your job is to bathe the leader in compliments, segue into how brilliant you are, and plant the seed in their mind that you should be next in line for a promotion and a pay rise.

Those of us incapable of slurping up to executives sit there, wooden and tense, smiling and nodding, taking discreet bites of our sandwich and hoping the salad does not lodge between our teeth.

However, we can learn a lot from these work suck-ups. The ability to say the right things to the right person at the right time is a good skill to have when a project goes pear-shaped or the wheels of promotion need a little greasing. But it requires sharp political skills to come across as sincere and not self-serving or manipulative. You need to be genuinely interested in other people, and pay attention to their responses.

What do the Stoics say?

Marcus Aurelius was attuned to the false compliments from sycophants eager to please a man in his powerful position. 'See how soon everything is forgotten,' he advised, 'and look at the chaos of infinite time on each side of the present, and the emptiness of applause, and the changeableness and want of judgement in those who pretend to give praise.' He knew, too, that the truth can be harder to determine when you're in a position of great power (see Rule 47).

'What is praise except indeed so far as it has a certain utility?' he asked. 'For you now reject unseasonably the gift of nature, clinging to something else.'

Yet others, like Fronto, seem to suck up to Marcus by comparing him to Julius Caesar when describing his ability to work under stressful situations:

'Gaius Caesar, while engaged in a most formidable war in Gaul wrote besides many other military works two books of the most meticulous character . . . On Analogy, discussing amid flying darts the declension of nouns, and the aspiration of words and their classification mid the blare of bugles and trumpets. Why then, O Marcus, should not you, who are endowed with no less abilities than Gaius Caesar, master your duties and find time for yourself not only for reading speeches and poems and histories and the doctrines of philosophers.'

Flattery fuels ego, and ego stalls progress, because it is impossible to improve when you are not open to honest feedback. Marcus knew that flattery was meaningless – and that believing the hype and allowing power and adulation to go to your head was dangerous. 'And here you must guard against flattery, as well as anger, for these are both unsocial qualities, and do a great deal of mischief.'

That is easier said than done. It is hard to dismiss the warm inner glow of being praised for a job well done, regardless of how authentic it is. Or to disregard someone else's delight at a compliment you have given them.

In *Meditations*, Marcus frequently reflects on the hollowness of fame and praise. 'Short-lived are both the praiser and the praised, and the rememberer and the remembered,' he observes. To live a good life, the Stoics advised self-reflection, practice and thought as virtuous pastimes. Praise itself is meaningless: 'Everything which is in any way beautiful is beautiful in itself, and terminates in itself, not having praise as part of itself. Neither worse then nor better is a thing made by being praised.'

A FINAL WORD FROM MARCUS AURELIUS

'People generally despise where they flatter and cringe to those they would gladly overtop.'
Meditations, 11.14

RULE 14

DON'T FREAK OUT

There's nothing like a misdirected message to bring on freak-out mode. You never remember the texts that you send to the right people. But the text about someone inadvertently sent to that person is forever burnt into your brain.

In a previous job, which I found tedious (I feel I should mention that some of my jobs have been excellent, others okay and some dire), we were sent an all-staff email from a leader about the previous month's achievements, how awesome the executives were – and that, of course, none of this would have been possible without 'our people', who were the 'foundation of our success'. I felt it my duty to forward this missive to a colleague with a note that said: 'The only thing this email didn't mention is how boring it is here – can't waaaaait to get out.' As you do. As soon as I pressed send, a flurry of responses came back. Turns out I had hit 'reply all', and my note went to everyone in the building. I spent the rest of the day frozen and crimson, wondering whether my career was over.

In the moments after you realise your error, your brain is in a state of disbelief. You retrace your steps, looking for clues that maybe it did not really happen. When reality sets in, you lurch into damage control and scramble to recall the message.

If it's an email, you could send a message recall notification – but that only encourages more people to pay attention to it. You could send out another note – but what would you write? 'Sorry I said this job is boring . . . It's not.' You could apologise to your boss and admit that you're having a bad day. In the end, no matter what you do, nothing can change what happened. You can either freak out or let it wash over you.

But what about when you wake up at 4 am with vivid, catastrophising thoughts about work? This is not the time to call or email anyone, or even to set up a meeting to resolve the problem. Instead, you should acknowledge that you do not have the resources in this moment to manage the situation. But you will soon, and things will seem much less catastrophic in the cold, hard fluorescent lighting of your office.

Remember, too, that other people in worse situations avoid freaking out. A woman who was the sole survivor of a plane crash in Vietnam that killed 29 others focused on the glistening sun instead of freaking out that the passenger next to her had worms coming out of his eyes. She kept her spirits up by congratulating herself when she found water. Six days later, she accepted that death was coming – and that's when she was rescued. Only after the event could she allow herself to freak out.

What do the Stoics say?

Marcus Aurelius was influenced by the teachings of Epictetus, who was well acquainted with the difficulties life could throw at you. Varying reports suggest he either acquired a disability from childhood, or his enslaver deliberately broke his leg. Early in his life, he became passionate about philosophy and studied Stoic philosophy under Musonius Rufus, viewing it as a way of life.

According to Epictetus, understanding that all external events were outside your control was the path to happiness and freedom. We can only control our thoughts, and our responses and reactions to external events. So these are the only things that should trouble us.

Such equanimity helped Marcus face wars, illness, treachery, and even the death of his children. Regardless of events, you always have control over your own mind.

Epictetus said: 'There is only one way to happiness and that is to cease worrying about things which are beyond the power of our will.'

Before freaking out, the Stoics would ask:

- Does getting upset provide me with more or fewer options?
- What if I see this as an opportunity rather than a disaster?
- Does what happened keep me from acting with courage, self-discipline, justice and wisdom?

If we can contain ourselves despite a monumental cock-up, then we can show restraint when something minor happens, because in the grand scheme of things it does not matter. What matters is keeping a cool head and resisting a meltdown.

A FINAL WORD FROM MARCUS AURELIUS

'Let these two maxims be always ready: first, that things cannot disturb the soul, but remain motionless without, while disturbance springs from the opinion within the soul. The second is, to consider that the scene is just shifting and sliding off into nothing; and that you yourself have seen abundance of great alterations. In a word, the world is all transformation, and life is opinion.'
Meditations, 4.3

RULE 15

JOLLY OTHERS
(AND YOURSELF) ALONG

One of the greatest pieces of work advice is to 'jolly people along' in order to get the best out of them. Bring a bit of fun to the workplace, some colour in place of the beigeness of working life. This works a treat, especially when workloads increase, deadlines loom and people become fractious.

At one workplace, we all paused at 3 pm to tell jokes, despite many of them being decidedly questionable. This followed a period of intense and gruelling work so the mid-afternoon lightness was much needed. They included:

1. What is blue and doesn't weigh much?
   Light blue.
2. Why did the toilet roll down the hill?
   To get to the bottom.
3. Knock knock.
   Who's there?
   Nobody.
   Nobody who?
   No body, just a head.

We had a whiteboard that we regularly filled with words we thought only wankers used:

- **PENCHANT**
- **VIS-À-VIS**
- **AUSPICES**
- **AS PER**
- **EVINCE**
- **VANGUARD**
- **VISCERAL**
- **PALPABLE**
- **APROPOS**
- **ENCHANTÉ**
- **METHINKS**
- **SYNERGISTIC**

We also set up a WhatsApp group where we shared funny names of people we encountered at work: Horatio Knobloch, Francis Bacon, Patti Bigbarge, Manuel Manibog, Donald Dickfos and Harold Onions, to name a few. The jolly-o-metre was dialled up to at least seven.

In order to create the conditions for jolliness, we have to attend to our own jolly levels. You do not need a fascinating or high-profile job that encapsulates your educational achievement to be happy, nor do you have to make a bucketload of money. (Though both these things help enormously, it has to be said.) Being a jolly person at work depends on your colleagues, the organisation's values, whether you feel a sense of accomplishment and whether there are freely available chocolate biscuits.

Jollying yourself and others along is not the same thing as positive thinking. It is an effective way to lighten the mood when things get heavy. This doesn't mean trivialising serious matters or being frivolous about dreadful situations. It lifts a tense atmosphere by sprinkling some lightness on heavy subjects, and gives everyone a break from relentless difficulty.

You can find a wealth of advice on how to be jolly, some of it absurd: just be funny, be happy, think positively and be true to yourself. That's a bit like telling someone to be Norwegian or become an astronaut. Some people are very jolly and others are not at all. Most of us are somewhere in the middle.

Looking on the bright side can bring some sunshine to the duller aspects of work. Being a little playful cannot lift a veil of drama, but it might provide a bit of relief. It can momentarily lull us out of difficulty and help make problems seem not quite so insurmountable.

What do the Stoics say?

The Stoics believed that using humour was a good way of managing the realities of a difficult world. As with most things, they encouraged moderate rather than excessive jolliness.

Seneca believed that things either made you laugh or weep, but it was much better to laugh than to lament. He was a big fan of laughing at ourselves, believing this was a kind of shield to our troubles and would help to lighten the mood. 'We must take a higher view of all things, and bear with them more easily: it better becomes a man to scoff at life than to lament over it,' he said. 'Add to this that he who laughs at the human race deserves better of it than he who mourns for it, for the former leaves it some good hopes of improvement, while the latter stupidly weeps over what he has given up all hopes of mending.'

Epictetus was also refreshingly witty, given the hardships he endured as a slave to the emperor Nero. 'I have to die,' he acknowledged. 'If it is now, well then I die now; if later, then now I will take my lunch, since the hour for lunch has arrived – and dying I will tend to later.'

RULE 15. JOLLY OTHERS (AND YOURSELF) ALONG

He was indifferent to criticism, laughing at anyone who thought they could damage him. 'If evil be spoken of you and it be true, correct yourself; if it's a lie, laugh at it.'

Marcus's writings suggest he was somewhat darker than other Stoic philosophers. If someone walked into the office with a combover and socks and sandals, I'm pretty sure he wouldn't have fallen about in a fit of laughter. The Stoics – unlike most people I have ever met – did not see humour in the misfortunes of others.

A FINAL WORD FROM MARCUS AURELIUS

'And as for that body that will not transmit the light, it will darken itself by resistance.'
Meditations, 8.57

RULE 16

PRETEND TO BE DISCIPLINED

There is a column in a newspaper weekend magazine called 'My Day on a Plate', in which people of note give a rundown of what they eat in any given day. Mostly, they start the day with lemon squeezed into water, followed by an egg white and spinach omelette, and for dinner a plate of activated air.

I start and end the day with chocolate, and generally wash it down with sauvignon blanc – with more chocolate as a reward for turning up to work. This is clearly an example of poor self-control, which I blame on the daily stresses of work.

Discipline means so much more than ticking off an unfeasibly long to-do list. It is also about resisting the temptations that are everywhere in life.

People who are very self-disciplined are not much fun. Their dedication to achieving their goals is quite annoying to those of us who lack their iron will, as they make us feel bad about our inability to see a task through to the end or get up at dawn to exercise in subzero temperatures. And yet without these people, nothing would get done.

We are living in strange times, and our resilience in recent years has been sorely tested. Hardships can help us grow if we let go of attachments and focus on what we can control. We have little control over most of our external circumstances, but we can control what we do and strive towards.

Self-discipline is the engine of progress and routine. No success, achievement or goal can be realised without it. It takes time to build up, but the rewards are rich if you can master it.

But if you cannot, you can always *pretend* to have self-discipline. 'Why kill yourself by working so hard when ultimately someone else will take all the credit?' a friend once said.

It is a cynical view, but a good one when it comes to not taking self-discipline too far. After all, it is not as though leaders are immune to lapses in discipline.

I've heard many stories of leaders not walking the talk. One friend said his global leader admonished the team for not adequately 'inserting the brand essence' into their work. 'He policed the brand like a hall monitor policed tardiness at school,' he said.

In a meeting, the leader grumbled at the team for not taking the brand more seriously. Someone stuck their hand up. 'Can you please give us an example of what we're doing wrong?' Another asked: 'Can you give us an example of what brand essence is?'

The manager looked at the team and shook his head. 'Nah,' he said. 'I can't be bothered.' Then he walked off, 15 minutes before the meeting ended.

'Not so disciplined,' my friend observed.

What's the answer?

'Pretend you are disciplined, but don't overdo it,' he said. 'That way, people will think you have the dedication of a well-paid senior leader when in reality you're not too bothered about whether work projects succeed or not. You'll do your best but not push too hard.'

It was really quite genius.

What do the Stoics say?

Self-discipline is an intrinsic part of Stoic philosophy. Marcus Aurelius believed it started with finding your purpose. A practical plan of action, with small and measurable milestones, helps us stay disciplined and progress towards an end goal.

'Guide your life towards a single course of action, and if every action goes its due length, rest contented,' he said.

Yet even Marcus seemingly got sick of the grind. He said in a letter to his teacher Fronto: 'For the last two days I have had no respite except such sleep as I have got at night: consequently, I have had no time as yet to read your lengthy letter to my Lord, but I greedily look forward to an opportunity of doing so tomorrow.'

Marcus spoke about voluntary hardship – that is, repeatedly testing ourselves by seeking out discomfort and hardening ourselves for when it becomes reality. Living within your means is a strategy Marcus embraced. He sold many of the imperial palace's furnishing to pay down his empire's debt because he did not need luxuries. The more things we desire and have to pay for, the less freedom and enjoyment of life we have.

'Do everything as a disciple of Antoninus,' Marcus said, referring to his adoptive father and predecessor as Roman emperor. 'Imitate him in the vigour and constancy of his good conduct, in the equality, sweetness and piety of his temper, the serenity of his aspect, his contempt of fame, and the generous ambition he had to be perfectly master of his business. Further, it was his way to dismiss nothing till he had looked through it, and viewed it on all sides.'

Taking a cold shower, eating two squares of chocolate instead of two family-size blocks, or choosing not to react when someone upsets you – each of these trains you for hardship.

Only people with mental fortitude and a sense of ownership, Marcus said, can steady the ship and keep going in the face of obstacles. 'Look upon the plants and birds, the ants, spiders, and bees, and you will see them all exerting their nature, and busy in their station. Shall not a man act like a man? Why do you not rouse your faculties, and hasten to act according to your nature?'

For his own part, Marcus looked for role models who embodied self-discipline, so he could learn how they mastered this skill.

A FINAL WORD FROM MARCUS AURELIUS

'Persevere then . . . the blazing fire makes flame and brightness out of everything that is thrown into it.'
Meditations, 10.31

RULE 17

DON'T COMPLAIN

A work friend complained to me about her own incessant complaining about work. She was worried because she was usually a raging optimist who saw the sunny side of things. While her glass was normally half-full, mine was generally empty. In fact, it wasn't even empty – there was just a puddle of liquid on the ground, with no vessel at all. Why? I resented the excessive meetings, the compulsory hot-desking, the lack of work boundaries and what would happen whenever things derailed.

In a former life, I worked as a television segment producer on a live TV show. It was my job one evening to look after three guests: a local soapie star, a Hollywood actor and a clown on rollerskates with a blue frizzy wig. The executive producer warned me that the soapie star had a tendency to drink when she got nervous: it was my job to make sure she did not get drunk. Meanwhile, I had to keep the Hollywood actor happy. I was given no instruction regarding the clown.

In the green room, the soapie star got drunk on three double Scotches before the interview. The Hollywood actor was grumpy because my focus was on the soapie star. The clown went missing. I searched the maze of rooms, but he had disappeared, never to be found again.

The executive producer complained that I had ruined everything. This was a stretch, I felt, given the show was not that great on a good day. But in response, I complained that the soapie star was an alcoholic, and this was clearly beyond my control. The Hollywood actor was temperamental and the clown unreliable. I complained some more and took no further responsibility. Then I quit. Instead of complaining, I should have taken responsibility, asked for more support for drunk, belligerent and unreliable guests, and viewed the incident as a 'learning opportunity' instead of whingeing and packing in the job.

Work is not always fun. Often it's filled with people getting things wrong and questioning you or disagreeing with you. Success means dealing with derailments, and not whingeing when things go wrong. But tedious projects, annoying people and impossible assignments are like springboards for serious whingers.

Whingeing about something will not magically change the situation, which makes the complaint pointless. This does not mean we have to stew in silence, though, and venting can help reduce the impact of a problem, even if a solution remains elusive. It's always worth investigating what's really behind a grievance, to better address the root cause.

What do the Stoics say?

Complaining is useless, according to Marcus Aurelius. A futile pastime. In his view, the matter is black and white. 'If it is not right, do not do it,' he says. 'If it is not true, do not say it.'

Marcus encountered many obstacles during his reign. His authority was challenged, he endured incessant warfare, many of his children died, and eventually his wife Faustina passed away. Even so, he said, worrying about other people prevented a person from doing what is useful. It is far better to act than to complain. We should focus on our own behaviour, not that of others.

As we saw in Rule 5, however, the Stoics were in favour of what we might call negative visualisation – which is good news for pessimists, because it gives them permission to imagine the very worst scenario as a way of preparing for when things go pear-shaped. There is a place for people who whinge in the workplace. Their role is just as important as that of those rare people who never have a bad word to say about anything.

'We are all cooperating to one great work,' Marcus said. 'The intention of the universal mind in the world; some, with knowledge and understanding, others, ignorantly, and undesignedly . . . One contributes to this one way, and another in another way. What's beyond expectation, even the querulous and the murmurers, who attempt to oppose the course of nature, and to obstruct what happens, contribute also to this purpose: for the world must have within it such persons also.' They provide an example of what not to do.

The next time I feel the urge to whine about the squelching sound my colleague makes as he eats his morning banana, I will imagine the worst. Like him going to the toilet, not washing his hands and then grabbing some M&Ms from the communal chocolate bowl (see Rule 20). Perhaps then the banana won't seem so bad.

A FINAL WORD FROM MARCUS AURELIUS

'Let no person hear you finding fault with the court life, or with your own.'
Meditations, 8.9

RULE 17. DON'T COMPLAIN

RULE 18

DON'T WEAPONISE CC

Email etiquette has been fraught since the dawn of online communications. For many of us, the shift towards remote working has made striking the right email tone even more important. People might not take you seriously if you are too friendly. Or they might be offended if you are not friendly enough. Sometimes you'll never know, as you anxiously await a reply that never comes.

Determining your tone starts with establishing the nature of the content and identifying your audience. How you write to a CEO is very different from how you write to anyone else. There are many decisions to be made. Do you start with writing 'hi' or 'hello' or 'dear'?

When you attain a certain level of seniority, of course you can be direct: 'Martin. Where is the PowerPoint presentation that's due today?'

Lower down the hierarchy, you do not have the luxury of omitting niceties: 'Hi Martin, I hope you had a great weekend! I was just wondering if you had a chance to look at the PowerPoint presentation that the CEO wants to see today? I know, crazy deadline! Let me know if I can help. Thank you!'

But regardless of where you are on the greasy pole of importance, being nice in emails pays off. Punctuation can help, but excessive use of exclamation marks is discouraged. Rarely do CEOs fire off all-staff emails that say: 'Profits are up!!!!' And how do you sign off? Cheers, cheerio, warm regards, thanks or yo?

One friend of mine said that life's too short for emails signed off with 'best', so she dispensed with email sign-offs altogether. 'It's so complex,' she sighed. 'I try so hard to be friendly in email (mostly) but so often I feel like it doesn't fly. Or I just get beige/vanilla back.'

The most controversial aspect of email etiquette is whether and how to CC other people. Some people weaponise CC to inflict reputational destruction. CC stands for 'carbon copy' yet it is a function that expanded beyond keeping third parties in the loop. It's become a tool for the kind of person at work who lets the boss know you've stuffed up by CC'ing all the important people. These are the type of people whose emails are intimidatingly timestamped 6 am or 11.30 pm to show their limitless capacity for work, in contrast to the person they are slagging off. Even sneakier is BCC (blind carbon copy) to show your co-workers how tough you are for roasting someone on email without them knowing that everyone else is in on it.

What do the Stoics say?

Marcus Aurelius used clear, direct and concise communication to express his thoughts. He was not known for levity or exclamations, or for excessive use of exclamation marks. Then again, he wrote *Meditations* for himself, and could not have known that it would become a self-help bible in the 21st century.

Marcus's tone reflected the tenor of his thoughts at the time, when as Roman emperor he was facing immense pressures and challenges: wars with the Parthian Empire, barbarian tribes on the northern border, the emergence of Christianity, a deathly plague, and a disappointing son and successor.

He advocated courteous, tolerant and mutually dignified social exchanges, regardless of the participants' social standing.

RULE 18. DON'T WEAPONISE CC

It is hard to imagine Marcus CC'ing senior leaders of his empire in order to denigrate or humiliate them. Then again, in his day there was no email and CC'ing meant keeping copies of letters.

Equally, the gravity of his philosophical insights would be lost if you add multiple exclamation marks. 'You shall sooner see a piece of earth refuse to lie by its own element, than find any man so perfectly unsociable as not to correspond with somebody or other!!!' No, it just doesn't have the same impact.

A FINAL WORD FROM MARCUS AURELIUS

'Here you must remember to proportion your concern to the weight and importance of each action. Thus, if you refrain from trifling, you may part with amusements without regret.'
Meditations, 4.32

RULE 19

DOUBLE-CHECK EMAILS BEFORE SENDING

A few years ago, I phoned into a meeting with a senior executive and my CEO. I had emailed them both a few minutes before the meeting began to say I could not attend in person because I was off sick.

It was my first meeting with the CEO since I'd started the job, and I was keen to make a good impression. The meeting went well, and after I hung up I basked in the warm thought of how well I'd handled the complex issue we'd discussed.

The next day, when I was back in the office, the senior executive from the meeting strolled over to my desk, leaned over and said: 'Do you realise your email yesterday said that you were "off dick"?'

It was mortifying – and the whole office knew about it. From then on, if I ever said I was feeling under the weather, my colleagues would ask if I was still off dick.

Fortunately, I was not alone. Typos are universal.

A graphic designer at a property company designed catalogues that showcased recent house sales. She put together a layout for one real estate agent, trumpeting his ability to sell 'nine out of ten properties in the last month alone'. Only she wrote 'none out of ten', deeply upsetting the agent, who did not care that the letters 'i' and 'o' are next to each other on the keyboard.

Another friend who worked on a Hong Kong newspaper was tasked with writing a headline for the front page. She thought she'd written: 'Hong Kong is back as market upturns' – until she saw the headline in print: 'Hong Hong is back as market upturns'. She moved back to Australia soon after.

What do the Stoics say?

Had the Stoics accidentally said the word 'dick' to a CEO, they would have shrugged it off. After all, we only have agency over our response to what we do and to the actions of others.

Keyboard fails soon disappear into the abyss of time. But some leave a lingering memory of cringeworthiness. Marcus takes a soft approach to those of us who stuff up. 'It is the privilege of human nature to love those who disoblige us,' he said. 'To practise this, consider . . . that ignorance is the cause of the misbehaviour and the fault is involuntary, and that you both will quickly be in your graves.'

It is such a fine line between being frazzled, bored and dissatisfied. But friction created by an email mishap can alert you to the dangers of fat fingers on keyboards – and make you more vigilant next time.

A FINAL WORD FROM MARCUS AURELIUS

'When you are troubled about anything, you have forgotten this: that all things happen according to the universal nature.'
Meditations, 12.26

RULE 20

DON'T EAT PRETZELS
ON THE TOILET

A colleague at work returned from the bathroom at work
perplexed. He had just heard someone munching on what
turned out to be pretzels on the toilet. The person holed up in a
toilet cubicle – a senior leader – was gnawing them like a squirrel,
taking several bites per pretzel while doing his business. Then his
phone rang and he answered. He was the ultimate multi-tasker.

My colleague was at the sink washing his hands when he heard
a flush and the senior leader emerged from the cubicle with an
empty pretzel packet. He nodded, dropped the packet in the bin and
walked out without washing his hands. News of this man's lapse in
the fundamentals of hygiene quickly spread through the office.

The next day, someone brought in some M&Ms and tipped them
into a bowl to share. The senior leader scooped up a handful as he
walked past. A message was pinged to the team, cautioning everyone
to steer clear of the M&Ms.

This story serves as a reminder to apply the same standard of
professionalism across all business activities, whether you're at your
desk, with a client, in a meeting or on the loo.

Toilet etiquette is fraught, mostly because there are many
unknowns. It's a roll of the dice who you will encounter when you
emerge from a cubicle. It could be a work pal, a stranger or the CEO.

Do you nod, say hi or give a knowing glance? Do you discuss work from your separate cubicles, or wait until you are both at the sink? If your colleague is engaging in big business, then do you scuttle out, hoping that no incoming person unfairly maligns you for any associated aromas? Or do you wait it out in the cubicle until you know for sure the coast is clear?

If someone is engaging in some hefty business and gets busted by colleagues afterwards, friends say that person is tainted until the end of time, regardless of their skill, talent or charisma. Basically, they need to change jobs.

What do the Stoics say?

The closest Marcus Aurelius comes to scatological advice relates to a joke he retold from the poet Menander about a man so wealthy and with so many possessions that he had nowhere left to empty his bowels.

'Now, what significancy and excellence can there be in these things, to which may be applied the poet's jest, that excess of luxury leaves no room for comfort?' he commented.

Marcus's son and successor as Roman emperor, Commodus, who was renowned for his simplicity and cowardice – and whose reign marked end of the golden era of peace in the Roman Empire – was murdered by Narcissus in a bathroom. He was strangled while taking a bath after an attempt to poison him went awry.

Perhaps he should have heeded his father's advice when he cautioned against bathing at strange hours. Marcus himself did not bathe for pleasure, only routine cleanliness.

Marcus advised viewing life as a spring of clear water that carries away dung and mud until it has washed itself clean. 'If you should throw dirt or clay at a spring, it would quickly disperse and the fountain will not be polluted,' he said. 'Which way now are you to go to work, to keep your springs always running, that they may never stagnate into a pool?'

His advice is to tap into our inner spring, to wash away negativity and keep our focus on virtuous improvement. One of the highest virtues, as he saw it, is to live in accordance with nature, as we are designed to do. 'Philosophy will put you upon nothing but what your nature wishes and calls for,' he said.

The next time nature calls, remember that it is not natural to eat pretzels while riding the porcelain bus. Especially in this era of global germs, it's best to wash your hands – particularly if your colleagues are nearby and a bowl of M&Ms beckons. Other than that, let the politics of the office toilet wash over you.

A FINAL WORD FROM MARCUS AURELIUS

'Tell me what you meet with in the business of bathing? There is oil and sweat, and dirtiness and water, but an offensive mixture, take it altogether. Why, life and everything in it is made up of such indifferent stuff.'

Meditations, 8.24

RULE 21

USE EMPTY PLATITUDES TO CUSHION NEGATIVE FEEDBACK

When I was 15, a teacher gave the following assessment of a history assignment I handed in: 'Overall, an effort was made.'

This was followed by less flattering comments about my work: 'Next time, don't try to jam the implications of both world wars into one sentence, as this results in the unpleasant task of having to read your work and it is not enjoyable.' I preferred the ambiguity of the first comment to the brutality of the second.

That moment taught me that empty platitudes can nevertheless have value. They certainly come in handy when delivering performance reviews for underperforming staff, or when giving a job reference to someone who is genuinely unemployable.

'Amazing is not the word' is how I described Terry to a recruiter. He was a grumpy journalist who had never mastered the art of writing, yet felt it his duty to tell others about his superior talents. Until he was sacked for incompetence. After he was fired, he rang me to ask for a reference. Then, when his job was advertised, he applied for it – which only reaffirmed the decision to let him go.

After that, he widened his job search to roles he had not been sacked from. A recruiter from a government department called for a reference check and wanted more details about Terry's approach to work. 'I've worked with lots of employees, and Terry was one of them,' I told him.

'What was he like to work with?' the recruiter asked.

'He was punctual and turned up most days.' I did not mention that when things got busy at work, Terry usually disappeared.

When the recruiter asked whether Terry was good at his job, I replied: 'He performed work and wrote sentences.' I believed this gave me sufficient coverage in the event Terry performed poorly enough to get sacked again. The recruiter could not accuse me of exaggerating his abilities.

Meaningless platitudes are also useful in performance reviews, the annual cycle of measuring output against a set of arbitrary goals, which are usually framed in such a way that failure is virtually impossible.

These days there are performance review generators online, which spew out inoffensive reviews for people of questionable talent. I typed in Terry's achievements and it supplied the following review: 'Terry was given many assignments and his performance defied measurement. His work greatly influenced the company and reflected a level of creativity not seen before. It would be accurate to say his impact on the office culture and dynamic was profound. The scale of his knowledge and values was unheard of.'

Of course, if I'd used this approach for Terry, he would have been rusted on to the company for the rest of eternity, so the review generator itself is clearly of dubious merit.

What do the Stoics say?

Our ability to accept feedback in such a way that we are neither dismissive nor offended by it depends, Marcus Aurelius knew, on how we view the person delivering the assessment. As for Marcus himself, he welcomed criticism. Recognising that everyone is flawed, imperfect and fallible makes interpreting feedback easier, because it gives more insight into the intentions of the person offering it. Taking the view that someone is trying to do the right thing is a great start. Moreover, we must make sure that we understand their approach before making a judgement about it – and that our own advice is offered in a helpful tone.

Marcus took guidance from his generals, teachers and senators, and encouraged honesty and 'plain speaking' at court. Decisions about his life and his rule therefore led to discussion and dialogue, and often criticism.

He strategically assessed feedback, which in his view, we have the choice to interpret either positively or negatively, and we can determine whether it originates from a place of good intentions or ill will. Feedback can be a learning opportunity when offered constructively and received with a positive mindset.

A FINAL WORD FROM MARCUS AURELIUS

'Monimus, the Cynic philosopher, used to say that all things were but opinion. Now this saying may undoubtedly prove serviceable, provided one accepts it only as far as it is true.'
Meditations, 2.15

RULE 22

DON'T GET CAUGHT SLAGGING PEOPLE OFF

It was a Friday afternoon and we were in a two-hour workshop. What better way to round off a tough week than spending 120 minutes of precious life discussing risk appetite, risk controls and something called a risk bowtie? (The last of these, it turns out, is not something you might wear to a dressy event.)

The host announced that he would share his screen, but as he fumbled with the settings, a manager's screen flashed up instead. On it was an email conversation between him and Leanne from business development, who had said about Jim from accounts: 'When are you hiring Jim's replacement?'

Until this moment, no one – including Jim – knew he was being replaced.

Making things worse was his manager's reply: 'Not soon enough.'

Jim looked pale and stared at the ground. The rest of us shifted uncomfortably in our seats and looked at one another. Jesus, there's no bouncing back from that, I thought. If I were Jim, I would be calling recruiters straight after the meeting. And if I were his manager, I'd be calling HR for help managing what was a monumental cock-up.

Eventually, someone told the manager that he was sharing his screen and that everyone in the room could read his emails.

He slammed his computer shut and acted like nothing had happened. The only giveaway that he'd stuffed up was his flushed neck. Then he mumbled something and went off to another meeting room, where we assumed he recounted to Leanne the horror of his faux pas.

Once you have slagged off an employee, a manager, a staff member or a customer and they hear about it, there really is no coming back.

Like the time Stephanie hung up after leaving a message for a customer. She turned to her colleague and said: 'You have to listen to his phone message – it's your classic monotone voice with no personality. He's obviously someone who does about an hour's worth of work a day. If that.' Only, she had not hung up.

In short, whenever you feel the urge to slag someone off on email, on the phone or in person – don't. Because it always gets back to them. And of all the people not to slag off, the executive assistant to the CEO is top of the list. Do not under any circumstances fall out with the CEO's EA. They wield disproportionate power and can make or break your career if you upset them (see Rule 13).

What do the Stoics say?

Since the dawn of time, people have behaved badly. Marcus Aurelius frowned upon those who slagged off others. But what if their behaviour is so egregious that you are compelled to knife them in the back? And what if you're the one being slagged off?

As we have seen, Marcus liked to commence each day by reminding himself that he would likely encounter 'the busybody, the ungrateful, arrogant, deceitful, envious, unsocial' that day. 'But I who have seen the nature of the good that it is beautiful,' he continued, 'and of the bad that it is ugly, and the nature of him who does wrong, that it is akin to me, not only of the same blood or seed, but that it participates in the same intelligence and the same portion of the divinity, I can neither be injured by any of them, for no one can fix on me what is ugly.'

Australian author and philosophy academic Matthew Sharpe explored extreme poor behaviour in his book *Stoicism, Bullying, and Beyond: How to Keep Your Head When Others Around You Have Lost Theirs and Blame You.* In his view, bullying in the workplace includes baiting, insulting, sidelining, demeaning and backstabbing, whether it's done by one person or a clique. If the target responds emotively, then the bully uses their response against them to claim they are unfit for their job.

According to the Stoics, there is no need to respond by showing fear, anger or despair. Stoicism advises that it is not what happens to us that matters, but how we respond to it. If there is justification in the criticism of us, we should learn from it. If the criticism is malicious, it reflects poorly on the proponent. If they spread untruths, then the information needs to be corrected. This toxic behaviour is about the bully, not the victim.

Stoicism reminds us that we have agency even if we are subjected to slander or unfair behaviour. We have control over our thoughts, feelings and actions, and we derive strength from our positive relationships with our family, friends and colleagues.

'Neither can I be angry with my brother or fall foul of him; for he and I were born to work together, like a man's two hands, feet, or eyelids, or like the upper and lower rows of his teeth,' Marcus said. 'To obstruct each other is against Nature's law – and what is irrational or aversion but a form of obstruction?'

A FINAL WORD FROM MARCUS AURELIUS

'If an antagonist in the circus tears our flesh with his nails or tilts against us with his head and wounds us we do not cry out foul play, nor are we offended at the rough usage, nor suspect him afterwards as a dangerous person in conversation.' *Meditations*, 6.20

RULE 22. DON'T GET CAUGHT SLAGGING PEOPLE OFF

RULE 23

MAKE A DECISION

I ndecisiveness can have profound consequences on people, businesses and the planet. Gareth, who worked in an engineering consultancy, could never decide when to take holidays, what work to assign his staff or whether to cut his hair. He ended up growing his hair long, which he fashioned into a ponytail and wore with a suit. His indecision thus had profound consequences for everyone else at work, because his colleagues were forced to look at his ponytail swishing about all day.

More seriously, indecisiveness can have profound negative consequences on a planetary scale – like dithering over climate change.

People who feel powerful are prone to poor decision-making, because they overvalue their own perspective, fail to recognise their limitations and dismiss the expertise of others.

Life is filled with hard decisions. As we get older, our decisions narrow our paths and our opportunities diminish. Big decisions force us to confront how to use the remaining time we have, which suddenly seems in short supply. Our genes, our childhood and the type of work we do all influence our response to the dilemmas we are confronted with each day. What desk to sit at, whether to say hi to Fiona from marketing or just give a cursory nod, whether to ask for a pay rise . . .

The neural patterns I have inherited from my parents, their ancestors and ultimately the Big Bang, it turns out, are behind my decision to eat a jam donut instead of looking at an Excel spreadsheet.

Good decisions can transform lives. Bad decisions are learning experiences (as long as we don't repeat them). And refusing to make a decision at all can leave you vulnerable to the decisions of others. That's why any decision, good or bad, is better than no decision. Dithering leads you nowhere. Progress doesn't happen without a decision.

A *Review of Economics Studies* paper by Steven Levitt, an American economist at the University of Chicago and host of the *Freakonomics* podcast, asked more than 20,000 participants to use a coin toss as a guide for their decision-making. After two months and after six months, those who had made a big change in their lives because of the coin's 'decisions' were happier and better off. As a result, Levitt advised always choosing action over maintaining the status quo. Someone agonising over a tough decision is likely better off choosing the option that leads to change.

What do the Stoics say?

Marcus Aurelius was known for taking his time to consider his decisions. But at least he made them, even though they were not always gold standard.

The Stoic decision-making process would be to consider what falls within your control. Anything outside of your control should not be your first priority. As Epictetus said, 'We are responsible for some things, while there are others for which we cannot be held responsible.'

A Stoic would also consider whether the decision embodies the four cardinal virtues designed to make us better human beings: practical wisdom (the ability to successfully navigate tricky situations), courage (to do the right thing), justice (behaving in the right way towards others) and temperance (showing self-control and restraint).

The Stoic flowchart for decision-making would go something like this. Firstly, ask yourself: is this under my control? If not, then there is no decision to be made here. Unless, of course, you have partial control of whatever it is you are deciding upon, in which case you need to focus on the bits you can control. And bear in mind that while the effort you put into the decision may determine the outcome, you ultimately do not control how things turn out.

A FINAL WORD FROM MARCUS AURELIUS

'If the gods . . . will take care of none of us, it is certainly lawful for me to take care of myself. Now, it is my right to consider my own convenience, and what is that? Why, that is convenient for everyone, which suits his nature and his constitution.'
Meditations, 6.44

RULE 24

HAVE A PURPOSE

Having a purpose helps get things done. Without it, we are aimless and flounder. Whether it is about meaningful change on a personal, professional or planetary level, purpose propels us towards a goal. My purpose or mission should not be to eat a family-size block of chocolate a day, even if my actions suggest otherwise. Rather, it might be to write about how to make work a better experience.

Purpose is not confined to people. Organisations have them as well. Some pay vast sums of money to consultants to devise a purpose for them – also known as a mission statement. These can be a powerful way to motivate a workforce to achieve a common goal. Amazon's statement is a cosmic vision 'to be Earth's most customer-centric company, where customers can find and discover anything they might want to buy online'.

Mission statements fall into three buckets: those that describe a company's actual purpose, those that include the phrase 'building a better world' and those that are downright ridiculous.

There was a flurry of excitement over the recent release of multinational firm Ashurst's five-word mission statement, which was formulated over multiple meetings with its thousands of staff, who were asked what it meant to be part of the company. It simply said: 'Together, we create the extraordinary.' The trouble with this was that it masked what Ashurst actually did. For all anyone knew, it might be a company that taught synchronised swimming or rescued injured otters. In fact, it was a law firm that charged for legal advice.

Good mission statements can be useful in focusing the efforts of staff members, and in making sure that their decisions reinforce what the company desires. They must be brief, ambitious and inspirational if they are to have an impact. And preferably grammatically correct and in touch with reality.

A decade or so ago, the US labelling and packaging company Avery Dennison's statement was very ambitious: 'To help make every brand more inspiring, and the world more intelligent.' That has inspired me to devise a mission statement for this book: 'To bring people and philosophy together to create an extraordinary working universe for all.'

The path towards defining your purpose is complicated by all the other statements companies must have. Employers with a purpose also have a vision, objectives, values and goals. On top of that, some companies embroider their purpose with other concepts, like a foundation, framework, scaffolding, planks, pillars, columns or grids. These supporting statements about how this ambition will be achieved generally only cause further confusion. Interestingly, the phrase 'I'm confused' is used often in the workplace as a polite way of masking actual rage that something has not been done properly.

To save themselves millions of dollars in consulting fees, companies could just fess up to their real purpose: to make money.

What do the Stoics say?

Marcus Aurelius looked for meaning and a broader purpose beyond the conveyor belt of a working life. He believed we were all created for a purpose – something that gets us out of bed in the morning – and it was our duty to carry it out. He didn't, however, use the phrase 'building a better world', or talk about moving his empire closer to the future or any other unattainable purpose.

If you have a clear understanding of your goals and the tasks you must complete to achieve them, then you are more likely to attain those goals. Having a reason is the biggest driver of self-discipline.

Marcus looked for deeper purpose and meaning in his work as emperor, and reflected on these each night in what became his book *Meditations*.

'Nothing is so likely to raise the mind to a pitch of greatness as the power truly and methodically to examine and consider all things that happen in this life,' he wrote, 'and so to penetrate into their natures as to apprehend at once what sort of purpose each thing serves.'

A FINAL WORD FROM MARCUS AURELIUS

'Do external things distract you? Then make time for yourself to learn something worthwhile; stop letting yourself be pulled in all directions. But make sure you guard against the other kind of confusion. People who labor all their lives but have no purpose to direct every thought and impulse toward are wasting their time – even when hard at work.'

Meditations, 2.7

RULE 25

DON'T SHAG THE BOSS

W hen asked what is the most important thing not to do at work, friends of mine said: Do not go to bed with the boss. Especially if they are not single. Of all the complexities we face as we navigate our working lives, this one tops them all.

On the one hand, it's a no-brainer. Romantic entanglements with a superior are fraught for those down the pecking order. Although it's deeply unfair, the power imbalance inevitably means the person lower down the work totem pole is disadvantaged or forced to leave the workplace when things turn sour.

On the other hand, well before that spark of electricity turns to romance, it is worth stepping back to focus on your manager's undesirable traits. The way they eat crunchy apples in earshot. How they peer over your screen to see what you're writing. The fact that they assign you unfeasibly large amounts of work, and never compliment you for a job well done.

Even so, office romances are common. A consultant once explained that the workplace created the conditions for amorous connections to flourish, because working is inherently stressful – we are dealing with difficult people, tight deadlines and complex problems. For some people, a psychological coping mechanism might be to sexualise stress in order to self-soothe and distract the mind. That's not to say love cannot blossom in high-pressure work environments. But it can be easy to mistake a sense of team cohesion for intimacy.

What's more, hierarchical workplace romances are more common than relationships between colleagues on an equal footing. Clearly there's something about the power the boss has that holds a certain cachet. Perhaps that explains how someone with a comb-over, zip-off pants and nasal hair might suddenly become so appealing.

What do the Stoics say?

The Stoics believed there were four passions that thwarted our progress. Future emotions are desire and fear, while present ones include pleasure and distress. Marcus Aurelius believed the source of our desire must be our principles and actions, which are within our control.

When it came to passionate desire, Marcus was no stranger to the hazards of the workplace romance. His wife Faustina the Younger was said to have had dalliances with young gladiators, who were the glamorous celebrities of ancient Rome. He nonetheless is believed to have remained devoted to her even after her death.

Marcus was guided by the critical virtues of temperance and justice. A workplace romance is not necessarily unvirtuous, but it can be when the action adversely impacts others. It is normal to desire things that are not good for us, Marcus recognised. Starting the day with leftover pineapple pizza (on the grounds that is fruit) is not living within the Stoical framework, but that did not stop me from doing it while writing this rule.

Epictetus also had much to say on the issue: our aim should be 'to live with desire and aversion (avoidance of certain things) free from restraint. And what is this? Neither to be disappointed in that which you desire, nor to fall into anything which you would avoid.'

A FINAL WORD FROM MARCUS AURELIUS

'But he that runs riot out of desire, being overcome by pleasure, loses all hold on himself, and all manly restraint.'

Meditations, 2.10

RULE 26

CHECK WHETHER CASUAL FRIDAYS ARE ACTUALLY CASUAL

There is nothing quite like that feeling when you wake up and realise it's Friday. That is, until you remember it's casual Friday. And the sartorial freedom of wearing whatever you want induces terror because of the pressure to look good in the office.

You rifle through your wardrobe looking for something casual but not too casual, cool but not too cool, and fashionable but not too fashionable. All you can find is a T-shirt with a giant pair of pink lips emblazoned on it and some orange corduroy culottes.

You do not want to take your lead from Rhonda from procurement and wear lime leggings with a crop top and high heels.

So, what do you wear? Obviously, it all depends on the tone of the workplace. Is it a place that reveres Hawaiian shorts, mandals and smocks? Or does casual mean a pair of Dolce & Gabbana jeans and a Chanel top?

When I made the leap from journalism to the corporate sector, I went from an office where dressing up meant wearing a matching tracksuit to one where dressing down involved Bottega Veneta shoes. On my first casual Friday in corporate land, I wore an old, crumpled white 'Choose Life' T-shirt, a wheat-coloured cardigan, jeans and some scuffed runners. Others wore Gucci, Dior and Valentino. They looked catwalk ready; I looked like I'd been putting out the rubbish bins.

You can learn a lot about a person on casual Fridays. The conservative economist who rocks up to work in orange platform runners and fluorescent-yellow parachute pants. The cool guy at work who wears a brown cardigan and slippers. Or Sharon from finance, who wears a dress with triangles cut out of it.

What do the Stoics say?

Marcus Aurelius grew up with tailored robes, which he wore in architecturally impressive buildings lined with masterful artworks. He was also a priest of the Salii, an order of priests who were devoted to ritual dance and worshipped Mars, the god of war. Marcus wore an embroidered tunic under a breastplate, a short military cloak and a felt hat of conical shape, and carried shields of figure of eight shape.

Yet he was also aware that possessions are transient, so there is no point getting too attached to them. All material objects – including clothing, which is purely material – were not objects to be desired.

Marcus outlined a technique in *Meditations* to examine the reality of what you desire. 'Where things appear most plausible, be sure to bring them to the test, and look at their worthlessness, and strip them of all the words by which they were exalted. Without this care, figure and appearance are great cheats; and when you think your fancy is best employed, you will be most fooled.'

When you covet high fashion, determine what you desire about it – is it the look or design? Or is it the social status attached to it, and the associated power?

Marcus evaluated a material item according to its physical properties – what it's made of rather than what others might think of it. This technique provides distance from our desire and our susceptibility to be dazzled by the superficial nature of designer clothing. This builds resilience against our whimsical desires for material things.

The next time Rhonda from procurement flaunts her Valentino shoes and lime leggings, be thankful you had the good sense to curtail your desire for one of the greatest fashion violations of all time.

A FINAL WORD FROM MARCUS AURELIUS

'He that can overlook his body will hardly disturb himself about the clothes he wears, the house he dwells in, about his reputation, or any part of this pomp and magnificence.'
Meditations, 12.2

RULE 27

DON'T GET (TOO) DRUNK AT WORK EVENTS

It is hard to know where to start with this rule. **On one level** it is obvious: getting sloshed at work events is a recipe for disaster. But there's also nothing better than getting sozzled with work colleagues and downloading on all that is wrong with capitalism, society and everyone you work with.

The trouble is that alcohol incinerates your inhibitions and can lead to conversations with senior leaders that can be somewhat career-ending.

Some decades ago, colleagues and I were invited to drinks at Parliament House. The couches were comfortable, the conversation interesting and the company engaging. My friend Caroline and I were both three days into our new jobs as political journalists, so we were keen to make a good impression. But as the champagne flowed, it became obvious that we were not exercising any moderation.

We found out that some MPs were holding a celebration out the back, which we merrily crashed. The couches were less comfortable, the conversation looser and the company a bit rowdier – largely thanks to us.

Things rapidly went downhill when Caroline accidentally knocked a politician off a verandah. He lost his footing and rolled down a few stairs to the grass, where he lay motionless. She then dragged me towards a minister, put our hands together and said, 'Here's your boyfriend.' Caroline then cornered another minister and outlined her own vision for the country. But her conversation was so garbled that he just copped a load of spittle in his face. She then shoved her empty glass in his face and said 'More wiiiiine!' He mouthed the word 'help' to his chief of staff.

The next day, our heads delicate and our reputations in an even more precarious state, we turned up to a media conference, where it became apparent that news of our misadventure had spread throughout the press gallery. Journalists and political staffers slow-clapped as we walked in. It will be no surprise that, just a few months later, both Caroline and I found ourselves in a regional court covering a case about a man who had married his goat, with our political aspirations lasting about as long as the man's marriage to his hoofed bride.

What do the Stoics say?

There is no evidence that the ancient Stoics did not have a drink or two. But it was all about moderation. Back then, too, it was considered barbaric if you did not water down your wine. The poet Hesiod – much admired by Marcus Aurelius, Seneca and other Stoics – advised a ratio of three parts water to one part wine. A moderate approach to alcohol rather than temperance. One that might, several millennia later, have spared an Australian government minister a face full of drunken journalistic spittle.

Seneca advised against getting sozzled as it undermines our capacity for judgement, which is a central Stoic virtue. And yet he also believed that drunkenness could be a remedy for mental anxiety.

The Stoics encouraged conviviality. Having a drink feels like it washes away our troubles, heals wounds and frees our mind from caring too much. But there is a difference between a couple with friends and eight shots at a work function. Seneca advocated a balanced life in work and leisure, including casual alcohol consumption.

'How much better it is to arraign drunkenness frankly and to expose its vices!' he wrote. 'For even the middling good man avoids them, not to mention the perfect sage, who is satisfied with slaking his thirst; the sage, even if now and then he is led on by good cheer which, for a friend's sake, is carried somewhat too far, yet always stops short of drunkenness.'

A little is fine – but not too much.

A FINAL WORD FROM MARCUS AURELIUS

'There is no living without rest. True; but nature has fixed a limit to eating and drinking, and here, too, you generally exceed bounds, and go beyond what is sufficient.'

Meditations, 5.1

RULE 27. DON'T GET (TOO) DRUNK AT WORK EVENTS

RULE 28

USE DEODORANT

Back in the 1980s, my mother founded a recruitment company that flourished in the pre-internet era thanks to her direct approach to managing people, clients and temporary staff. Her army of casual workers were sent out on short-term contracts with various corporate clients, and for the most part things went smoothly.

But occasionally there was a hiccup. Like the time a client rang Mum to complain that one of her casual workers had a serious body odour problem. They wanted her to deal with it, otherwise they did not want that worker back.

Her name was Anastacia and she was well presented except for her pungent body odour. Mum brought her into the office and delivered the classic shit sandwich: 'Anastacia, you are doing a great job. Everyone loves your work. There's just one small issue – it would be fantastic if you could wear some deodorant. For the benefit of your co-workers. Other than that, everything's going really well!'

It was a conversation that would today cause HR serious headaches. Anastacia's reaction was to burst into tears. She called her boyfriend, who rushed to the office and confronted Mum. The problem was not his girlfriend – she smelled just fine, he insisted.

Mum nodded politely until they left. 'The trouble was, he stank as well,' she said later.

Anastacia and her BO returned to the office, and the employer moved her to a desk with no people around. They also placed a 'group can' of deodorant in the communal area, should anyone feel the urge to freshen up. Anastacia left soon after. It was, in numerous ways, a different era.

These days the matter needs a softer, more delicate touch, given the potential legal ramifications. You need to be kind and set expectations about personal hygiene. Offer the person time and space to address the issue. Take notes, in case it does become a legal matter. And when choosing a meeting room to discuss the issue, make sure there's a window that opens.

What do the Stoics say?

As we know by now, one of the central Stoic principles is to focus on things that are within our power, and to stop bothering about things that are not. Clearly it is within our control to take care of our BO in the workplace.

You start the day fresh and full of anticipation. By the end of the day, unexpected and stressful detours can leave you smelling less like a daisy and more like a teenager's bedroom. This was no different during Roman times. Marcus Aurelius spoke about washing away the dust of earthly life.

In *Letters from a Stoic*, Seneca touches on cleanliness in the context of hard work and cautions against luxuriating in extravagant bathhouses. He cites the example of the Roman general and statesman Publius Cornelius Scipio Africanus, who was instrumental in Rome's victory against Carthage in the Second Punic War. Scipio used the cramped, dark bathhouse in his farmhouse to wash his weary body. He bathed infrequently to wash off the sweat and toil after a hard day's work. He didn't have the luxury of a shower as they didn't exist.

So perhaps, if you're a hard worker, a bit of BO might be okay.

A FINAL WORD FROM MARCUS AURELIUS

'Wash yourself clean. With simplicity, with humility, with indifference to everything but right and wrong.'
Meditations, 7.31

RULE 29

DON'T BE UPSET BY CONSTRUCTIVE CRITICISM

Bill was tasked with writing a speech about capital management systems for a senior executive. The speech was to be delivered at a drinks function, so it needed to be light-hearted and preferably funny to engage the crowd. No problem, Bill said to his boss. A funny speech about capital management. Coming right up.

'I'm doomed,' he later moaned. 'How do I make capital management systems light and engaging?'

'It'll be fine,' I reassured him. 'Everyone's going to love it.'

They did not. The speech fell flat as a tack. The response veered between indifference to mild unkindness. 'My dog Harold could have given a more interesting speech,' one audience member was overheard saying.

Bill was deflated. But why? He had delivered against a difficult brief – and anyway, who had ever made capital management systems light and breezy?

Still, this was just one piece of constructive criticism. It could be worse – much worse. There are companies looking at 'continuous development evaluation', the idea being that you receive instant feedback on everything you do at work. Rather like that episode of *Black Mirror* where people are rated on a scale of one to five for every interaction they have as they go about their day. The rating system impacts their socioeconomic status and behaviour, so naturally everyone scrambles to boost their ratings, with disastrous consequences.

When you get feedback, especially after things have gone pear-shaped, the quality of the person delivering it is everything. Are they someone with integrity and insight? If so, their feedback is a gift. Or is their mission to kneecap your confidence so they can swim across the rip of your misfortune and secure their own success?

I once received some feedback from a boss via yet another accidental email meant for a peer that lobbed into my inbox saying I was 'unnecessarily chaotic'. I was offended and vowed to quit immediately. Until I realised that he was right. Take my handbag, for instance. It is filled with loose Maltesers, lipsticks with no lid, a poncho in case it rains (as well as an umbrella), a bag of chicken-flavoured cat treats, a squash ball even though I don't play squash, used vouchers for beauty treatments, mittens even though it may be the height of summer and face masks smeared with lipstick. Everything but my actual wallet, which I inevitably leave at home. This does not suggest someone who glides through their work and life with military precision.

So yes, my boss was right. I am chaotic. But I dispute that I am unnecessarily so. I am necessarily chaotic in order to juggle work and life, just like everyone else. Anyway, I left that job too.

What do the Stoics say?

Marcus Aurelius embraced useful information or advice, studied those he admired, and welcomed anyone who could show him a better way of looking at things. He challenged other people's views where necessary and accepted criticism from others.

Instead of dismissing the criticism that is not valid, the Stoic response would be to pause before reacting and check your thoughts. The person delivering the criticism might think the

RULE 29. DON'T BE UPSET BY CONSTRUCTIVE CRITICISM

statement is fact rather than feedback, so take time before responding − and do not lash out. When we think someone has criticised us, we must remember that it is just their opinion, and we should not get upset about that, because it's beyond our sphere of control.

If Marcus wrote a speech on capital management systems that fell flat, he would likely keep in mind that the negative reactions would lose their sting if he was not offended by them. Often, people criticise in order to get a reaction, but if there is no response, the attack loses its potency.

Getting upset by the opinion of someone you do not know or respect is like finding tomatoes upsetting (which they sort of are, actually). But it is good to invite feedback from those whose views you respect. Self-reflection, ignoring unfounded criticism and embracing constructive feedback are vital to self-improvement.

A FINAL WORD FROM MARCUS AURELIUS

'Not every one's good opinion is not worth the gaining, but only that of those who seek to live in accordance with Nature.'

Meditations, 3.4

RULE 30

TRAIN LIKE AN ATHLETE TO TACKLE APPROVALS

To work is to face adversity. It is everywhere in modern life. From the cup of milky dissatisfaction masquerading as a morning coffee that costs upwards of $5, to the photocopier that needs a new cartridge when you have just two minutes to get a printed report to the CEO.

One of the biggest tests of adversity is getting work approved. Around the time that Stoicism was founded by Zeno, a Roman navy was formed, trained and mobilised against the Carthaginians in 260 BCE. This took just 60 days – a fraction of the time it takes to get a one-page brief approved in the modern working world.

The approvals process is a bit like moving house – in that at first you think, *How bad can it be?* By the end, you're exhausted and demoralised.

The whole process goes like this.

You start with a nice piece of work – succinct, informative and maybe even a little creative.

At this point you send it to Gary, the IT subject matter expert (or SME), who inserts 50 lines of technical twaddle. 'This makes no sense,' you say. He gets upset, so you compromise and only cut half of it out.

Next up the document goes to Nathan from legal. He adds the phrases 'we seek to' and 'we aim to' before every sentence.

Bob from the executive office is next to 'hold the pen'. He seizes on a sentence that says 'Our business sees a solid outlook in the year ahead' and is indignant. He adds the comment: 'Does our business have eyeballs? Can it really see?'

'No, Bob, it cannot,' you reply.

Someone suggests that an image be dropped into the brief of an auditorium with empty chairs. You push back. Another adds initial capitals to words that don't need it – Company, People, Workforce and Operations. You change them all back to lower case.

Rhonda from procurement gets her hands on the brief. She adds the phrases 'unpack the issues', 'high-level examination' and 'shift the dial on customer interface'.

Now Bob comes back, adding two quotes that say nothing, and suggests we include the company purpose of 'building a better tomorrow by moving the business closer to the future'.

That is scientifically impossible, you reflect.

Gary is now worried that the brief has lost its technical edge, and slices out the last of the comprehensible bits, replacing it with jargon. After two months of 'development', the brief ends up looking like a turd. It is a mess of incomprehensible information.

Athletes inoculate themselves against stress before high-pressure situations to make sure they conserve their energy, and those of us who must push documents through a maze of approvals should do the same.

What do the Stoics say?

The Stoics were masters at managing setbacks. Conditions were brutal in the middle period of the Roman Empire, and the Stoics did not wallow in self-pity when faced with difficulties. Indeed, they relished adversity, believing it made them stronger.

Marcus Aurelius might acknowledge that getting approvals in the workplace is like swimming in glue. Then again, he would know that how we respond is the most important thing – not why Gary is insisting on transforming a brief from adequate to terrible.

Like most Stoic philosophers, Seneca faced significant adversity in his life. As a Roman senator, he was ordered to commit suicide by Caligula, only to be saved by severe illness that was expected to kill him anyway. He survived, but was later sentenced to death by the Senate – only to have this commuted to exile by Claudius. After working as an adviser to Nero, Seneca was ultimately forced to take his own life. 'Sometimes even to live is an act of courage,' he said. Sometimes even to turning up to work is an act of courage.

Seneca said that the more we persevere under adversity, the stronger we become. His philosophical insights into adversity included gems such as: 'Constant misfortune brings this one blessing: to whom it always assails, it eventually fortifies.'

'Virtue alone affords everlasting and peace-giving joy; even if some obstacle arise, it is but like an intervening cloud, which floats beneath the sun but never prevails against it,' Seneca said. He advised not to give in to adversity and guard against 'premature ambition', which could 'result in great personal and public misfortune'.

> **Seneca reminds us that instead of avoiding challenges, we should face them head on, and not let setbacks discourage our progress.**

Adversity improves performance and builds resilience, forcing us to grow and explore new ways of managing the problems we encounter. Seneca reminds us that instead of avoiding challenges, we should face them head on, and not let setbacks discourage our progress. We become

'antifragile' and thrive when confronted by obstacles. 'I judge you unfortunate because you have never lived through misfortune,' Seneca said.

Seneca himself faced adversity until the very end, never relenting. 'No tree becomes rooted and sturdy unless many a wind assails it,' he said. 'Difficulties strengthen the mind, as labour does the body.'

A FINAL WORD FROM MARCUS AURELIUS

'To be vexed at anything that happens is a separation of ourselves from nature, in some part of which the natures of all other things are contained.'
Meditations, 2.16

RULE 31

DON'T RESIST CHANGE

No one likes change. I am still upset that fun-sized Mars Bars are now an unfun microscopic size. Worse is the struggle since the coffee shop near work used the pandemic as an excuse to no longer include those little biscuits with my cappuccino.

Work is all about change. From new jobs to new tasks, new people – we are in a perpetual state of change. One minute you're working alongside funny, witty, helpful colleagues. The next you're sitting beside someone called Shelley who has the annoying habit of saying 'ah' after every sip of tea. Things can change on a dime.

In corporate land, there is a whole industry devoted to change. Swarms of consultants charge millions of dollars to reshape organisations to make them more efficient. Buzzword-laden reports are produced, with phrases like 'critical pathways', 'deliverables' and 'drill down'.

Even if your company has not been taken over, corporate restructures are deployed with such regularity that it is hard not to wonder whether this is done to keep lining the pockets of the burgeoning 'change management' industry. A former colleague who worked for some years in the insurance sector said restructures were unveiled on a yearly basis. 'By the time you worked out what was actually going on, another restructure came along, so in the end we were none the wiser as to how to do our jobs,' she said.

Sometimes change creeps up on you, and you only realise things are different when you look back. Other times it is more overt – such as when groups of workers are made redundant.

The only thing worse than being sacked is reading about how companies describe axing staff. British former *Financial Times* columnist Lucy Kellaway wrote about an investment management company that described sackings as going 'into the gym . . . inducing cell renewal and thus making the company fit for profitable growth'. Another company announced it was 'demising' certain roles. A third said, somewhat shamelessly, 'We look forward to strengthening our alumni network.'

Change is inevitable. So is communication that makes change sound far better than reality. And as the Stoics knew, if you cannot personally change something, there is no point in you worrying about it.

What do the Stoics say?

Marcus Aurelius viewed change as inevitable. He wrote that everything will change in an instant, and what we know now will no longer exist in future because the universe is change.

Things you fear or desire may happen at any time. Yet amid life's volatility, your mind can be the stable force. 'Has any advantage happened to you? It is the bounty of fate. It was all of it preordained you by the universal cause, and woven in your destiny from the beginning,' Marcus said. 'On the whole, life is but short; therefore be just and prudent, and make the most of it.'

Stoicism contains many practices to give us this perspective. These include *memento mori*, to help us reflect on our own mortality; *praemeditatio malorum*, to help us prepare for setbacks; and *amor fati*, to love only what happens, what was destined.

'Motions and changes are continually renewing the world, just as the uninterrupted course of time is always renewing the infinite duration of ages,' Marcus said. 'In this flowing stream, then, on which there is no abiding, what is there of the things which hurry by on which a man would set a high price? It would be just as if a man should fall in love with one of the sparrows which fly by, but it has already passed out of sight. Something of this kind is the very life of every man, like the exhalation of the blood and the respiration of the air. For such as it is to have once drawn in the air and to have given it back, which we do every moment, just the same is it with the whole respiratory power, from when we first drew it at birth to when we give it back to the element.'

If a restructure at work is about as appealing as a mosquito buzzing around your ear at 3 am, acknowledge that you have no power to change the situation. Your power is to control your own response to it. Marcus would acknowledge that change was taking place and also that he resisted it – as this acknowledgement could be a source of solace.

Our brains are hardwired to resist change. Yet we require friction – in the form of discomfort or change – to propel ourselves forward. Change takes us off autopilot and fires up the engine of progress.

Marcus delineated between an objective event and an emotion attached to it, in an effort to transform feelings of misfortune into motivation. Knowing the difference between a shift in circumstances and the emotion it stirs is the key to our ability to cope with change. That is what can turn setbacks into success.

A FINAL WORD FROM MARCUS AURELIUS

'The world subsists upon change … What it loses one way it gets in another.'
Meditations, 4.2

RULE 31. DON'T RESIST CHANGE

RULE 32

HAVE A SIDE PROJECT

Work is not and should not be everything. Most jobs have limited scope for creativity, and they dominate our waking hours. Finding meaning takes time – yet time is in short supply when you must work.

Australian newsreader and journalist Juanita Phillips wrote a book in 2010, a period when she was busy juggling a full-time job and toddlers. It was called *A Pressure Cooker Saved My Life*; the tagline on the back of the book read 'A baby + a toddler + full-time job = total meltdown'.

Phillips concluded you could have it all, but not at the same time. Her secret weapons were a pressure cooker and the concept of 'time squeezing'. This is where you tackle a particular task, such as writing a book during the brief interludes between other tasks – as you wait for dinner to cook, for example. Clearly, this approach enabled her to have a side project.

The ideal side project is something that restores your energy and gives you an identity away from your work. Find whatever it is that floats your boat – Irish dancing, planetary poetry, playing the pan flute, birdwatching, collecting those dolls you see in horror films, metal detecting, macramé or writing a book – and insist on doing it.

Brainless scrolling, eating a family-sized bag of salt and vinegar chips and binge-watching TV are lovely (and addictive) pastimes, but they do not count as side projects. They offer only fleeting hits of dopamine that punctuate the decades we spend toiling away.

A former colleague felt defeated when he thought about his lifetime of soul-sucking work drudgery when all he wanted to do was write a book. His would be about bleakness, he told me. The main character would wistfully wander a windy, desolate beach, weighed down by despair and hopelessness. It would be a riveting read, he insisted . . . although he had not yet started. Because writing a book is not like gliding through water. It is more like wading through a swamp at night, with no torch and no idea about the dangers ahead.

Too much time spent in frenetic but shallow activity erodes our capacity for deep work and creativity. The trick is to apply the structure and external motivation that work provides to your side project.

Being able to switch between focus and daydreaming is an important skill, but it is curtailed by constant busyness. Engineering scarcity into our days can free up time for creative thought. Many important discoveries were made during downtime. Nikola Tesla had an insight into rotating magnetic fields while walking in Budapest. Albert Einstein liked to listen to Mozart during his breaks from intense thinking sessions.

Salvador Dalí believed he got a creativity boost during the early stage of sleep, when reality gets mixed up with fantasy. To use the technique, Dalí would hold an object, such as a spoon or a ball, while falling asleep in a chair. As he drifted off, the object would fall, make a noise and wake him up. Having spent a few moments on the brink of unconsciousness, he would be ready to start work.

What do the Stoics say?

Marcus Aurelius led a dance troupe that recited obscure chants and performed a military dance in honour of Mars, the god of war (see Rule 26). The College of the Salii, where Marcus was a priest, trained youths for the athleticism of battle.

'The art of life is more like the wrestler's art than the dancer's, in respect of this, that it should stand ready and form to meet onsets which are sudden and unexpected,' he said in *Meditations*. He was also known to hunt, play ball sports and wrestle – and, obviously, to dabble in philosophy as he built the traits that made him suitable for later office and caught the eye of the Emperor Hadrian.

As emperor himself, Marcus faced constant time pressures. But instead of wallowing over an unfeasibly long to-do list that was barely touched by the day's end, he would reframe his thoughts about his job and his achievements. Maintaining a creative project gives you a sense of agency. Instead of feeling defeated by the monotony of working alongside people you would not save from a burning car – or, at the very least, would not have a beer with – a creative project concentrates your mind in areas you can control.

Seneca's drama *Medea* is a creative work that teaches Stoic values with an ethical purpose. Creative works that are more ethically neutral, such as an abstract painting or music, contribute to our soundness of mind, and therefore our soundness of character.

Littering the mind with creative works that lack this quality is a choice, and the Stoics would likely classify celebrity news and chocolate as vices, not virtues. But is virtue combined with a little vice so bad? Giving the brain a break from deep thinking might even ignite a creative spark. That is my justification anyway, if I accidentally find myself reading the 'sidebar of shame' and creatively stuffing my face.

A FINAL WORD FROM MARCUS AURELIUS

'But those who love their several arts exhaust themselves in working at them unwashed and without food.'
Meditations, 5.1

RULE 32. HAVE A SIDE PROJECT

RULE 33
TAKE A COSMIC PERSPECTIVE

To prisoners, the sky is freedom: they can look up beyond the confines of the walls and see the unattainable expanse that stretches beyond their limited realm.

From the confines of our beige office walls, the sky also takes on greater significance. Listening to Sharon from finance talk about the importance of the stakeholder ecosystem, I focus on the glimpse of blue visible though a high window. Sharon often eats a bag of nuts, one by one, during meetings she hosts. I have found the sky a good distraction when small flecks of nut project from her mouth as she complains about Tom from HR. The sky does not care that Sharon is early in her 'personality and people skills journey'.

When the alarm goes off early on a Monday morning and my mind turns to the week ahead – crammed with work, meetings and Sharons – it can seem overwhelming. That's when I like to look up at the pre-dawn sky and marvel at its vastness. Work cannot encroach on this spectacle of Jupiter and Venus shining in the lilac dawn.

This telescopic perspective on life can make whatever is troubling you seem insignificant. When you think about stars, galaxies, black holes the size of half the universe – even the possibility that we're living in a multiverse – you realise that pride, frustration and an intolerance of people who eat nuts and spit fragments at you while telling you to circle back make no sense. We are microscopic specks in a grand cosmos.

Even so, there are times when a little space from certain colleagues is a welcome thing.

What do the Stoics say?

The Stoics used a technique called the 'view from above'. This means stepping back from whatever is troubling you and considering the world from on high, so as to strip away trivialities and gain a better perspective on life. Thinking about our place in the cosmos shows just how inconsequential Sharon – and all the rest of us – really are.

Marcus Aurelius said that much unnecessary trouble stems from our own judgements, which means 'you may free yourself from it when you please'. He advises his readers to 'take the whole world into your contemplation, and consider its eternal duration and the swift change of every single thing in it. Consider how near the end of all things it is to the beginning! But then the ages before our birth and after our death are both infinite and immeasurable.'

The truth is we are not insignificant in the grand scheme of things. The fact that we are here, part of the cosmos, actually makes us incredibly significant. But our status, our reputation and our personal insecurities are infinitesimally small concerns amid the vastness of space and time.

Marcus also examined our place in the world by breaking things down into their constituent parts. 'Continually study the history of nature and trace the progress of bodies from one form and species to another, contemplate often upon this subject, for there is nothing contributes so much to greatness of mind,' he wrote.

The Stoics believed in a living cosmos. For them, everything stemmed from the *logos*, a divine logic or reason. The cosmos, as they saw it, was a singular, living entity, of which insects, people, planets, clouds and oceans were intrinsic parts. That view made humans just a fragment of the universe, which remained indifferent to our worries and concerns, whether that's a meeting with no outcome, an unreasonable customer or a colleague who complains she's busier than everyone else.

The astronaut Edgar Mitchell said: 'In outer space you develop an instant global consciousness, a people orientation, an intense dissatisfaction with the state of the world, and a compulsion to do something about it.'

And of course, no one can hear Katie's baby voice or Sharon's singing in the vacuum of space.

A FINAL WORD FROM MARCUS AURELIUS

'Look round at the courses of the stars, as if you were going along with them; and constantly consider the changes of the elements into one another.'
Meditations, 7.47

RULE 34

DON'T SQUANDER TIME

Life is shockingly short. As we get older, it accelerates like a film reel on fast-forward. The weekend whizzes past, and in the blink of an eye we are back at our desks, responding to a passive-aggressive email from Leanne in business development, who has CC'ed the CEO and the board of directors. Just as time slows down near a black hole, it crawls along in meetings. Meeting time drags about twice as long as normal time. Normal time lasts about four times as long as weekend time. And weekend time is about eight times as long as holiday time.

The British writer Oliver Burkeman, in his book *Four Thousand Weeks*, pointed out that if we make it to 80, we only have about 4000 weeks to spend on Earth. That's an unsettling idea, when you think about the amount of time you squander on pointless activities. So far, I've spent about 50 weeks reading online froth, probably twice that watching rubbish on TV, and even more procrastinating about doing things like pairing odd socks, tidying up or writing this chapter. Sometimes, time seems to disappear into the ether.

Reminders of time are ever-present in the office: on computers, on calendars, on phones and in meeting rooms. Time violations are deeply frowned upon.

People respond in different ways to disappearing time. Some melt under the burden, while others are professional delegators and leave the rest of us suckers to do their actual work. As we saw in Rule 11, some people only work when the boss walks past their desk – the classic 'sensor light'. The rest of the time they watch cat videos on YouTube or day-trade to pass the time.

The secret appears to be to embrace the unknown – and to accept that time is not yours to spend how you see fit. Our ultimately doomed efforts to control the future reveal the limitations of time. We simply cannot influence the future. The only time within our reach is the present.

What do the Stoics say?

Marcus Aurelius ruthlessly guarded his time, reserving space for himself to think, to analyse and to ponder life's big questions. His disciplined focus meant that he would not be easily distracted.

He wasted little time after the death of his adoptive father, Antoninus Pius, securing the loyalty of the Praetorian Guard (the emperor's personal bodyguard) and the armies with largesse. This ensured his reign for longer than other later contenders, such as Didius Julianus, who was beheaded when the bribe he offered for power was not forthcoming. Amid military campaigns and political turmoil, Marcus made time to write in his journal, which became *Meditations*, to make sense of the power plays that threatened to cut short his reign.

As Marcus saw it, procrastination was a squandering of our most precious resource. The philosopher Seneca agreed: 'We're tight-fisted with property and money, yet think too little of wasting time, the one thing about which we should all be the toughest misers,' he said.

Delaying anything 'snatches away each day as it comes and denies us the present by promising the future', Seneca wrote. The 'greatest obstacle to living is expectancy'. Seneca believed we had plenty of time in which to notch up a few achievements in life if we put in the effort. Life is only short if we squander the opportunity to do something of note with it.

So how best to avoid dithering or delaying actually doing something when it needs to be done? Resisting any mindless distractions or low-priority chores like cleaning the skirting boards or decluttering the sock drawer. Preparing ahead of time for potential issues that might stall a project helps you push ahead and overcome obstacles.

Time is an irreplaceable asset – we cannot buy more of it. We can only strive to waste as little as possible, because in the end, as Marcus says, the 'abyss of endless time swallows us all'.

A FINAL WORD FROM MARCUS AURELIUS

'Time is like a river made up of the events which happen, and a violent stream; for as soon as a thing has been seen, it is carried away, and another comes in its place, and this will be carried away too.'
Meditations, 4.43

RULE 35
SAY NO

One Friday morning, Tim sent a message to a group thread – a cry for help. He was drowning in a mountain of work at his construction management job. When he explained to his manager that his workload was unfeasibly large, his boss told him to continue on regardless because it was a 'step up opportunity' to prioritise and be more efficient.

'So he leaves me drowning in excrement,' my overworked friend said.

Tim said he usually began each week with a sense of hope that things would somehow be different, and his work would become a place of satisfaction, hope and advancement. But by the end of each week he felt more cynical and despondent than ever. He shared his weekly psychological state, which went something like this:

MONDAY: Ahh, fresh week – let's get that bread.
TUESDAY: Oh. Okay. That was a curve ball. This week is not going to plan, but let's bounce back.
WEDNESDAY: Today I figured out how long it would take me to learn to code, so I could just work from my basement and never interact with anyone for the rest of my life. And I could use alcohol to numb the pain.

THURSDAY: I hate this company and everyone who has ever contributed to it. Should I leak some shit about them to the media?
FRIDAY: Okay, let's just get to 5 pm and then I'll reassess my life on the weekend.
WEEKEND: Think about anything but work.

Tim's main issue was an unrestrained workload, caused by a boss who underestimated the time it took to get through a mountain of work. 'I've been holding the fort on my own since two colleagues left,' Tim explained. 'I get vague and lumpy oversight from my boss. But whenever something goes wrong, he hides.' The solution for Tim was to just say no.

Another gift the pandemic delivered was career burnout for many people as the boundaries between work life and home life blurred. Workloads increased when working from home – but then remained there when office life resumed.

The solution? Impose clear work boundaries, and when these are crossed then just say no.

Author Oliver Burkeman argued that saying no created space and energy, and that saying yes should be reserved for things that really matter. Also, 'No.' is a complete sentence. There is no need to overexplain why you said no. Just say it politely, briefly justify why the boundary is necessary, then move on.

But remember: saying no doesn't always work. Will Smith turned down the role of Neo in *The Matrix* so he could make *Wild Wild West*. Also in the late 1990s, Yahoo squandered billions in future earnings when it turned down an offer to buy Google for $1 million.

 ### What do the Stoics say?
When you feel pressured into saying yes to another work request, Marcus Aurelius would advise that you focus on what is necessary and discard things that are not essential.

'For the greater part of what we say and do, being unnecessary, if this were but once retrenched, we should have both more leisure and less disturbance,' he says.

We should consider why we blindly agree to things. Is it out of vanity, greed or fear? Or do we wish to seem agreeable when really the right answer would be no?

Marcus uses the Greek word *euthymia*, which is usually translated as tranquillity but also means staying on a path without distraction. That means stepping back and not being a slave to meetings, calendars, invitations and requests that, when it comes down to it, don't matter.

'Be sure you entertain no fancies, which may give check to these qualities,' Marcus says. 'This is possible, if you will perform every action as though it were your last; if your appetites and passions do not cross upon your reason; if you keep clear of rashness, and have nothing of insincerity and self-love to infect you, and you do not complain of your destiny.'

A FINAL WORD FROM MARCUS AURELIUS

'You see what a few points a man has to gain in order to attain to a godlike way of living; for he that comes thus far, performs all which the immortal powers will require of him.'
Meditations, 2.5

RULE 36

KEEP EXPECTATIONS LOW TO AVOID DISAPPOINTMENT

As a child, when someone asks what we want to be when we grow up, we usually aim high – prime minister, inventor of a cure for cancer, triple gold Olympian. Then, as you get older and your possible career paths narrow, you settle for something more modest – strategic stakeholder adviser, IT manager, regional relations coordinator. Then, when you reflect on your career, you wonder: Should I have gone bigger? Did I aim too low?

Maybe not. Having low expectations means you are rarely disappointed. Expect that some commuters on the train will have forgotten to put on deodorant, that the only desk left is next to Rhonda from procurement, and that Steve from partnerships will appear from yonder and glide past and say, within earshot of everyone, that the report you did was rubbish.

Expectations need to be calibrated to the situation. I listened to a senior member from NASA's shuttle program give a talk on safety and the events that led to the *Challenger* and *Columbia* disasters. Clearly, in such instances, expectations on safety need to be sky-high. But when I delivered a PowerPoint presentation recently on how to create communication value (step one: don't use the term 'communication value'), it froze on the title slide and I slipped into sheer panic. But this was clearly not proportional to a shuttle-like disaster and did not deserve the stratospheric worry when things did not go according to plan. Even though the audience stared at me awkwardly as I failed to unfreeze it, the situation was just a momentary and forgettable blip that ultimately impacted no one. I should probably have expected a stuff-up at some point so that I was unsurprised when it did happen.

Unreasonable expectations steer us into unhealthy directions, because they set us up for failure and open us up to criticism from ourselves and from others. You feel you should perform perfectly at your job, which is impossible. This might discourage any risk-taking. Lofty aspirations assume a level of control that we do not necessarily have in a situation, and do not allow for flexibility or changed circumstances.

When he suffered a stroke, the poet Walt Whitman told himself to 'tone your wants and tastes low down enough, and make much of negatives, and of mere daylight and the skies'. He edited his expectations so they were in line with his new reality, and sought joy within these new parameters.

That's why I lowered my expectations when I walked up to Steve's desk to ask him about encouraging commercial partners to put a presentation on their social channels. He told me he was extremely busy and then put a timer on his phone for two minutes. When it buzzed, he asked twice if I had anything further to say. 'I forgot to tell you this morning you've had a piece of spinach in between your front teeth all day – sorry,' I said.

What do the Stoics say?

Unmet expectations in matters that are outside our control leave us vulnerable, fragile and disappointed. The Stoic practice of negative visualisation – contemplating the worst-case scenario in advance – is a better alternative than daydreaming about unattainable fantasies. This technique helps us navigate tricky scenarios should they arise, and prepares us for the worst.

The Stoics would tap into their wellspring of resilience and resourcefulness to confront whatever reality occurs, instead of conjuring fanciful ideas of how things should unfold.

Marcus Aurelius said: 'For as the universal nature overrules all mutinous accidents, brings them under the laws of fate, and makes them part of itself, so it is the power of man to make something out of every hindrance, and turn it to his own advantage.'

Develop a mindset in which you limit expectations beyond reasoned choice, and give no power to external forces over which you have no control. Rigid expectations attached to a fictional path only set us up for disappointment when they do not translate to reality.

'He is a madman that expects figs on the trees in winter; and he is little better that calls for his children again when they are dead and buried,' Marcus said.

Stoicism sees that we are only harmed when our character is affected, or when we let our standards slip. While it is not ideal to stuff up a presentation or lose a job or fall out with a co-worker, our character remains intact and we still control how we respond. Lower expectations help us manage our response to disappointment.

A FINAL WORD FROM MARCUS AURELIUS

'Leave these unnatural changes and commotions to those fickle men, who thus change, and are changed. Be intent upon this: how to make good use of such events.'
Meditations, 7.58

RULE 36. KEEP EXPECTATIONS LOW TO AVOID DISAPPOINTMENT

RULE 37

LISTEN MORE

I t was Friday, and the last online meeting of the day had dragged on for an hour. Everyone was lost in a fantasy about the drink they would guzzle immediately afterwards to revive their souls, which had been depleted by 60 minutes of discussion about a new sales system.

As the meeting came to an end, our hopes were dashed when Rhonda from procurement asked a question: 'Can we please go through the next steps one more time to make sure we action them appropriately.'

There was an inescapable sense of disappointment on everyone's faces. Because we all knew that Rhonda asked questions that were not, in fact, questions. They were really just a segue to her own thoughts on the work universe.

In this case, we were lectured about the importance of meetings and how they are a forum for discussion and debate. There was no mention of action items or any outcome. The only reason people listened was that they were on camera, and so were forced to nod politely as they waited for the right moment to leave. But no appropriate pause came.

So the only thing to do was to interrupt her. 'You raise some good points about meetings, Rhonda,' I began, 'but back to the sales system . . .'

Then Rhonda interrupted me to say she hadn't finished. Then the host interrupted her to say we'd run out of time to set the next steps. Rhonda kept talking anyway. And one by one we just dropped off the meeting until she was left talking to herself.

The exchange revealed that most of us never really listen to anyone, except to wait for a brief pause in the conversation so we can steer the conversation back to ourselves. Most advice on managing interrupters relates to young kids, but adults are really the worst offenders.

Had Rhonda actually listened to her colleagues with a receptive mindset, she might have avoided the humiliation of being ghosted before the meeting had even ended.

What do the Stoics say?

The Stoics encouraged intentional listening to others, with the aim of empathising with them so that we really understand what they are saying. This also means resisting the urge to speak, even if we feel compelled to add something.

Zeno, the founder of Stoicism, famously said: 'The reason we have two ears and only one mouth is so we might listen more and talk less.'

In any discussion, our aim should be to listen most of the time, and to contribute only when we can offer something that is genuinely worthwhile. Which rules out most work waffle.

Marcus revered his adoptive father, Antoninus Pius, and said that 'listening to anyone who could contribute to the public good' was one of his many admirable qualities. Marcus advised that we listen to those 'whose lives conform to nature'. Nature has multiple meanings in Stoicism: it can mean the universe in which events occur; natural functions, or the process by which livings things are created, change and die; or the ability to reason in order to better grasp the logic of what is good, bad or indifferent. Most importantly, nature equates to virtuousness.

RULE 37. LISTEN MORE

All of this suggests that Marcus would not spend too much time listening to Rhonda from procurement blab on about meetings in a meeting. And the others? He would bear in mind what sort of people they are – both at home and at work, by night as well as by day – and with whom they spend their time. And listen if they had something of genuine interest to say.

He not only listened but considered what was said from other people's perspectives when he said: 'Accustom yourself to attend carefully to what is said by another, and as much as it is possible, be in the speaker's mind.'

A FINAL WORD FROM MARCUS AURELIUS

'Do not let either discourse or action pass unobserved; attend to the sense and significance of the one and to the tendency and design of the other.'
Meditations, 7.4

RULE 38

DON'T EMPLOY TOXIC PEOPLE

If all employers heeded this advice, then most workplaces would be much happier environments. But they don't. Which means that no matter where you work, there will always be a Workplace Voldemort.

A recent WV was Leanne from business development. She had a brown bob, a scratchy voice and a psychopathic smile. Once her target had been identified, she arranged events for everyone but the target to attend. She then circulated message debriefs about how great the event was and how well the team had bonded.

During meetings, she would say, 'Well, we've all been waiting patiently for you to do your job,' while her target sat there squirming. She'd arrange a team coffee but 'forget' to invite her target, and in the mornings she'd walk into the office and greet everyone but the person she decided needed to be frozen out. She was your basic nightmare.

A WV does not reveal themselves to anyone upstream – only to peers and others lower down the flagpole. In their eyes, they are hardworking, agreeable and full of goodwill. To a target, they are manipulative, ice-cold and full of mind trickery. The only way a leader can discover they have a WV in their team is to talk to everyone on the team. Trouble is, no one wants to slag off the WV in case he or she is mates with the leader, and the complainer then ends up in the organisational deep freeze.

It is impossible to screen for VWs during recruitment, because they have probably blackmailed their referees to say nice things, lied on the personality test, and discoursed glowingly during the interview about their people skills and desire to nurture their team. The only way to get a peek behind the curtain before they come into your workplace is to get them to the pub and let the alcohol strip away their inhibitions. When they start slagging off perfectly nice people, then you know you have a VW on your hands.

What do the Stoics say?

Enduring what we cannot control and changing what we can – such as which people we surround ourselves with – are central pillars of Stoicism. It is easy to slag off a toxic peer, but in doing so, we become just as mean. When there is a choice to remove these people from our orbit, it means we are choosing to put our attention elsewhere.

Marcus Aurelius refused to accept the top job as Roman emperor unless the Senate conferred equal powers on his adopted brother, Lucius Verus. During the nine years they were co-emperors, Marcus was believed to be unimpressed by his brother's debauchery and involvement in frivolous activities like gladiatorial games and hunting (see Rule 1). In the end Marcus may have had some hand in Lucius's death as they travelled together across the Alps.

Marcus took guidance from Epictetus, who said: 'It is inevitable if you enter into relationships with people on a regular basis that you will grow to be like them . . . Remember that if you consort with someone covered in dirt you can hardly avoid getting a little grimy yourself.'

Who we surround ourselves with matters. At work, we should give our attention to those who want to become wiser, kinder and more fulfilled. They cultivate virtue by encouraging and supporting us, and can provide valuable feedback. If a toxic person cannot be spring-cleaned from your working life, however, then you should – where possible – minimise the oxygen you give them.

How we respond to toxic people and to discomfort and misfortune helps us build resilience and better endure future challenges. Marcus asked himself if he had been harmed by the problem person, and resisted the impulse to respond rudely. Ultimately, the best response is to go high when they go low.

A FINAL WORD FROM MARCUS AURELIUS

'The best revenge is not to be like that.'
Meditations, 6.6

RULE 39
EMBRACE TEAM-BUILDING DAYS (NO MATTER HOW EXCRUCIATING)

Team-building exercises are for employers. Not employees. For those of us in the trenches, they can feel like time-wasting rituals of torture that force us to spend intensive periods with people we would much rather not. Unless they are done well. In which case they are highly valuable love-ins that can instil harmony and insight in the working organism.

When an invitation for a team-building day lobs into the inbox, the first ritual is for staff to roll their eyes and complain about all the work they cannot get done. There is usually a psychometric test to complete beforehand. It asks questions like: 'Do you like working alongside people?' No. 'Do you hold back when someone at work wrongs you?' No. 'Do you wish you won Lotto so you didn't have to work?' Yes.

On the day, it is a good idea to have a friend on standby, who can call you with a fake emergency just before the session in which you and an arbitrarily chosen team build a sculpture from uncooked spaghetti and marshmallows. If that fails, you can just fake your own death during the 'get to know your colleagues – energiser' session. Either that or engage in a conversation with work strangers about everything and nothing – mainly nothing, as your only common ground is your employer.

Then there is the part of the day when the facilitator hands out the results from the personality test. The numbers 1 to 10 are placed on the floor from one end of the room to the other. Everyone is instructed to stand on the number that corresponds with their results across several personality attributes, such as introversion or agreeableness.

When the facilitator tells everyone to move to the number they scored for self-control, most people congregate somewhere in the middle. They look around and see you at the end of the room, standing on your own on number 1, and gasp.

'Are you even employable?' someone asks.

What do the Stoics say?

Detecting gravitational waves. Discovering breakthrough medicines. Harnessing the potential of quantum technology to tackle climate change. These things happen because people work together to solve complex problems. Yet it is a challenge to get people to work well together. Unrestrained emotions can destabilise the social connections that are necessary if teams are to achieve great things.

Marcus Aurelius endured his fair share of toxic people, and a distinct lack of cooperation from people who wanted to deceive or murder him. Yet he thought of the universe as a 'single living being', and believed we are all an intrinsic part of something larger.

'As you are a member of society yourself, so every action of yours should tend to the benefits and improvement of it,' Marcus wrote. Elsewhere he put it more succinctly: 'That which is not good for the swarm, neither is it good for the bee.'

Seneca, too, spoke about our interconnected nature, saying: 'Our fellowship is very similar to an arch of stones, which would fall apart, if they did not reciprocally support each other.'

Acting in harmony with nature benefits not only others but ourselves, according to Marcus. This means we must endure working with the likes of Leanne, Steve and Sharon to build a pasta tower, even if we would rather be at home rearranging our sock drawer.

A FINAL WORD FROM MARCUS AURELIUS

'Men exist for the sake of one another. Teach them then or bear with them.'

Meditations, 8.59

RULE 40

KEEP EXPECTATIONS LOW WITH PRESENTATIONS AND SPREADSHEETS

O n 20 April 1987, a piece of software was born that had the twin effects of both slowing down time and inducing mind-numbing boredom during early-afternoon meetings and conferences.

Done well, a PowerPoint presentation can inspire, invigorate and maybe even change the hearts and minds of audiences, and win over investors. But cram a presentation with enough words, images, bullet points, charts and infographics, and it's more likely you'll transport the audience into a vortex of tedium. One that not even the flashiest slide transition can resurrect. Our will to live slips away as the bullet points scroll by, the 'SmartArt' flies in and the supposedly funny graphics bounce into view.

Presenting is no walk in the park. There's always that moment when you fumble about trying to get the slide deck to start working but the screen is blank. You apologise and madly press any button, before looking for IT assistance somewhere in the audience, but everyone is sitting in uncomfortable silence. Or maybe you forgot to turn off your notifications, and an email from a friend appears: 'Is your boss still being an a-hole?'

Imagine the impact Martin Luther King would not have had if he had accompanied his 'I have a dream' speech with a list of bullet points. Or if Winston Churchill had been standing in front of an infographic map as he indicated where we would fight the invaders.

Even more divisive are Excel spreadsheets. Like coriander, you either love or loathe them. For the less numerate, try juggling a pivot table, a macro and formulas that come up with an error message when you input a number, and soon you're making desperate calls to Gary from IT on a Friday afternoon when your budget is due. The spreadsheet is a sea of ########## and 'VAL error' messages – whatever that means. Mostly, the numbers just don't seem to make any sense. How did you end up needing a $1,023,543 budget for stationery next year?

Back in the 1970s, the spreadsheet was just for engineering and finance teams. It has since become ubiquitous, inflicting a world of pain on everyone but those odd souls who are devoted to it. Whenever I am asked in job interviews about my weaknesses, I freely admit PowerPoint and Excel – which may explain why I never get the job.

It's useful to remember that neither PowerPoint nor Excel will bring joy to the workplace and that anyone who loves them must have something wrong with them (no offence).

What do the Stoics say?

What would Marcus Aurelius have done if he found himself fumbling with a frozen PowerPoint presentation or losing a chunk of money from his budget because he'd accidentally erased the formula on a spreadsheet? His Stoic training would instruct him to view such obstacles as opportunities to improve.

Marcus practised managing his own perceptions during challenging situations. Instead of being stricken with fear as his IT failed him, he would focus on what he could control. He would consider his own response to the situation, and would likely not bash the keyboard in a panic.

Marcus refused to allow himself to be rattled by things he could not influence, which is a fundamental Stoic principle. He took responsibility for his own work, and didn't relinquish power in situations beyond his control.

'When any accident happens,' he advised, 'call to mind those who have formerly been under the same circumstances, how full of surprise, complaint and trouble they were about the matter. And where are they now? They are gone – their murmuring could not make them immortal.'

A FINAL WORD FROM MARCUS AURELIUS

'And this was not God's will, in order that my unhappiness may not depend on another.'
Meditations, 8.56

RULE 41

DON'T BOAST ABOUT WORK ON SOCIAL MEDIA

Believing that your talents at whatever job you do are unmatched by other mortals is one thing. Boasting about it on social media is another. Megaphoning your good professional fortune on social media channels is unwise on so many levels because of the high risk that it will backfire.

Like the bloke who posted on Instagram a photo of himself at the races with a simple two-word caption: 'loving work'. He was a high-profile adviser to a prominent politician, and being in a corporate box at the races contravened his party's policy on receiving gifts. His political career came to an end once the media got hold of the story.

Bragging about your professional accomplishments is no better. Yet dozens of posts on social media start with the cringeworthy phrase 'I'm so proud of . . .', followed by a blatant brag about an achievement. Sometimes the phrase 'I am so humbled . . .' is used instead, but there's no humility in broadcasting your wins on social media. Sharing news of your achievements is only ever useful if you provide some meaningful insight for the audience.

The ultimate – combining a work post with a holiday brag – is most potent in the dead of winter, when the grim weather has depleted everyone's spirits. 'Hey from sunny Hawaii!' you write. 'Had a great strategy meeting followed by a surf, and then on to cocktails and bonding with the strategy team!' Without any detail about what the workshop produced, such a post falls squarely in the 'so what' category.

Steve from partnerships once shared a picture of himself accepting an award for 'partnership excellence', which he'd won the night before, with the caption 'I shouldn't have accepted this award – my team should have been there' and a sad face emoji. He was congratulated by his superiors, but congratulations from his subordinates were conspicuously absent – because he hadn't invited them.

What do the Stoics say?

Humility is a driving force of Stoicism, because without it our ability to learn, adapt and build relationships is undermined by pride. Epictetus said: 'It is impossible for a person to begin to learn what he thinks he already knows.'

Marcus Aurelius lived a humble existence, saying only what was necessary and never chest-thumping and back-patting himself for his achievements. He let his actions speak for themselves. 'Nothing is more scandalous than a man who is proud of his humility,' he observed.

Elsewhere, he said: 'A fleet horse or greyhound does not make a noise when they have done well, nor a bee neither when she has made a little honey. And thus a man that has done a kindness never proclaims it, but does another as soon as he can, just like a vine that bears again the next season.'

Our acts, he believed, should be driven by our desire to help others, rather than in search of recognition, praise and adulation.

'Remind yourself that your task is to be a good human being; remind yourself what nature demands of people. Then do it, without hesitation, and speak the truth as you see it. But with kindness. With humility. Without hypocrisy.'

A FINAL WORD FROM MARCUS AURELIUS

'Receive wealth or prosperity without arrogance; and be ready to let it go.'

Meditations, 8.33

RULE 42

MINIMISE DESK CLUTTER

What you have on your desk says a lot about you – and about your approach to work. Are you someone who covets minimalism and maintains a sterile wasteland with nothing but a keyboard, mouse and monitor on your desk? Or do you squander precious minutes each day looking for your keyboard under a pile of fluorescent post-it notes, old printed reports, *Star Wars* Lego figurines, one of those waving lucky cats, several staplers and a pile of binders you will never use?

I used to have a snow dome collection at work that included the Eiffel Tower, a moped from Italy and an alien from Area 51. But hot-desking plays havoc with work ornaments, which have to be packed away each night in your locker and rearranged on your desk the next morning.

Some workplaces enforce a clean desk policy. From one point of view, this is a sensible move to deter hoarders from making the workplace look like a teenager's bedroom. But on the other hand, it strips away any means of expressing your personality – and contravenes the philosophy of 'bringing your whole self to work' (see Rule 46).

Some argue that when our desks are a hot mess, so are we. Fruitlessly searching for lost items impedes clear thinking, decision-making and even work relationships. Visual reminders of disorder are a cognitive drain, they say, and we are more productive when we keep a tidy desk. Cluttered desks may even result in poor eating choices and make us more stressed. Desks piled with empty coffee cups, old reports and discarded papers makes us appear less than conscientious. A daily tidy-up and regular spring cleaning will restore our image as a hard worker.

One defence of messy desks is that they can spark creativity. Pristine environments, some say, promote conformity and maintaining the status quo, and so might discourage creative thinking. As with everything, some middle ground seems to be the answer. So maybe choosing just three snow domes to display each day instead of rolling out the full 25 could be the answer.

What do the Stoics say?

The Stoics viewed clutter as a distraction. Marcus Aurelius glorified the virtues of the simple life, a view shared by Seneca. 'One needs no silver plate, encrusted and embossed in solid gold,' said the latter. 'But we should not believe the lack of silver and gold to be proof of a simple life.'

Seneca's position on snow domes remains unclear. But the simplicity he advocated applied not just to physical objects but also to our thinking, with the aim of finding peace of mind. When we remove the fog of physical and mental clutter, it is easier to focus on what is important to you and how best to get your job done. It seems clear that Marcus found journalling to be a soothing exercise that helped him empty his mind of concerns and work through any worries he was having.

A powerful teaching of Stoicism is to curtail our desire to accumulate things: we should consciously avoid wanting more of everything. Cluttering our brains and our environment makes us a slave to our desires. When that happens, no matter how much we get, we will always want more.

Epictetus said: 'Wealth consists not in having great possessions, but in having few wants.' There is power, too, in making use of what you already have. 'Cure your desire – don't set your heart on so many things and you will get what you need,' he argued.

So it appears the Stoics would be in favour of the clean-desk policy . . . but then they also promote creative thought, so perhaps a slimmed-down snow dome collection might pass the Stoic test.

A FINAL WORD FROM MARCUS AURELIUS

'The greater part of your trouble lies in your fancy, and therefore you may free yourself from it when you please.'
Meditations, 9.32

RULE 43

REMEMBER, WORK HAPPINESS LIES BETWEEN FEAR AND BOREDOM

Australian columnist and author Jane Caro wrote about the continuum between boredom and fear, saying a man named Arthur North 'brilliantly defined happiness' as sitting somewhere on this spectrum. Where it was located differed for everyone, and for different aspects of life. Some felt happiest when their lives were predictable and comfortable – closer to the boredom end. Others preferred a bit more fear and excitement.

My equilibrium sits somewhere closer to fear, but not too much. Moving from journalism to the corporate world pushed me further towards this end of the spectrum because of the seismic unfamiliarity of this new universe.

In journalism, each day promised an unknowable future: events might lead you to a bushfire, a parliamentary hearing or an interview with a fallen CEO. Even so, the uncertainty about how each day would unfold was nothing compared to the people, the language, the clothes, the sights, the sounds and even the smells of the corporate sector.

The newsroom was a featureless expanse, so large that the meeting room where the editorial direction was set each day was obscured by the curvature of the Earth. Before the mass redundancies, the atmosphere fizzed with tension, excitement and ambition. The air smelled of damp carpet, instant coffee and deadline pressure.

In corporate land, people wore designer clothes, the language was baffling (see Rule 3), the kitchen was stocked with orange juice, cola and bar snacks, and the air was filled with wafts of Chanel No. 5. The atmosphere was vibrant, friendly but complex. You needed to know how to play the game. Allies were critical to your survival, as was talking the talk, adhering to the weird rules and corporate 'values', engaging in some subtle self-promotion and, most importantly, drinking the Kool-Aid of your company's mission.

Friction is a critical ingredient in the alchemy of workplace happiness. There are uncontrolled variables that influence your disposition at work. Being paid well for your talents, having a sense of accomplishment, receiving recognition for a job well done and having a work–life balance are all vital for a happy worker. Moral and philosophical alignment with your employer, and having a leader who does not overload you with work and gives you the space to actually do your job, helps too.

The American writer Arthur C. Brooks advises that striving for happiness will bring success, but the formula does not work in reverse. Success does not necessarily bring happiness. In my experience too, focusing on finding happiness at work will make you more productive and more attractive to employers, and – all going well – will bring you success.

What do the Stoics say?
People with the most meaningful jobs can suffer paralysis at the thought of another day in the office. Rather than greet the day with enthusiasm and vitality, we press snooze five times until it no longer works, and fantasise about doing a Ferris Bueller and just taking a day off.

Marcus Aurelius advised that we should perform our duties in a way that is governed by reason; you should 'manage what lies before you with industry, vigour and temper; if you will not run out after a new distraction, but keep your divinity pure . . . then you will be a happy man. But the whole world cannot hinder you from doing so.'

He believed it was in our nature to live a life of service – to help others and contribute to the world. Any resistance to this natural imperative would mean rejecting our purpose in this life.

The Stoic version of happiness hinges on cultivating a good and rational mental state that is in harmony with nature, and on adopting a calm indifference towards external events.

A FINAL WORD FROM MARCUS AURELIUS

'In a word, happiness lies all in the functions of reason, in warrantable desires and virtuous practice.'
Meditations, 5.36

RULE 44

EAT WITH CAUTION

Eating in the workplace is fraught. So much so that some ban eating at your desk altogether. The sight, the smell and the sound of a co-worker eating a blue cheese salad with croutons is enough to test anyone's resilience, and impede productivity.

Yet eating lunch at your desk can be one of the greatest pleasures at work! You can work uninterrupted and without the pressure of having forced conversations with colleagues in the communal kitchen.

The offline world has moments of mini drama. Entering and exiting the kitchen means you will inevitably cross paths with the person you least want to speak to. Leanne from business development picking at a chicken salad, one lettuce leaf at a time, or Steve from partnerships putting away an egg sandwich, bits of mayonnaise caught in the corners of his mouth.

If you were working from home, you would just close your computer and head for the fridge in colleague-free comfort. In the work kitchen, you have to negotiate your way past others and apologise when you both reach for the fizzy water tap.

In person, you must ensure that your lunch can be eaten quickly, efficiently and with minimal sound. Bringing to work a lunch that needs assembling opens you up to a revolving door of conversations with Gary from IT and Kristy from projects, who operate with military precision and tolerate no one for being substandard in the workplace.

Eating crackers in the middle of a meeting or a saucy sandwich that leaves smears on your face or a bean salad that makes your tummy gurgle or a tabouli salad that lodges in your teeth will get you plenty of unwanted attention. This is why I eat fun-sized chocolate bars for lunch – minimal fuss and minimal opportunity for chitchat.

What do the Stoics say?

Unsurprisingly, the Stoics favoured simple food – nothing too fancy. Marcus Aurelius regarded food as fuel, and ate healthily and quickly. There was no indulgence in rich food or expensive wine.

How and what we eat is an opportunity for self-discipline. The Stoics ate a lot of grains and vegetables, and saved time each day by eating simple meals that did not require much preparation. Instead of gorging on cake daily, they would take a moderate approach and indulge weekly. Eating a diverse diet composed of healthy food provides the foundations for a healthy life.

Antoninus Pius, the adoptive father of Marcus Aurelius, minimised his bathroom trips thanks to a simple diet, which allowed him to engage in longer stretches of uninterrupted work. Seneca believed a good diet minimised the need for exercise and freed up precious time for the practice of philosophy. They did not gorge on pretzels or peanut M&Ms for an afternoon fix.

That's not to say snacking was frowned upon. In fact, it was part of the routine. Epictetus had some solid advice about banquet etiquette, which reflects how we should behave in life. Basically, don't hog the food.

RULE 44. EAT WITH CAUTION

'Remember that you ought to behave in life as you would at a banquet. As something is being passed around it comes to you; stretch out your hand, take a portion of it politely. It passes on; do not detain it. Or it has not come to you yet; do not project your desire to meet it, but wait until it comes in front of you. So, act toward children, so toward a wife, so toward office, so toward wealth.'

The Stoics approached their food mindfully and artfully. When they ate meat, they considered its origins, and how it came to be on their plates, instead of mindlessly devouring whatever was laid out before them.

I imagine the Stoics ate very discreetly. They would not inflict the smell of boiled egg and fish on anyone nearby, or ostentatiously eat a crunchy apple at their desk so others heard every bite with clarity.

A FINAL WORD FROM MARCUS AURELIUS

'When the hearing and smelling are in good condition, they do not pick and choose their objects, but take in all manner of scents and sounds. Thus a strong stomach despatches all that comes into it, like a mill that grinds all sorts of grain.'

Meditations, 10.35

RULE 45

BE LIKEABLE, BUT NOT TOO LIKEABLE

Raymond was the obituary writer who incited fear in everyone in the workplace. He was intense and spiky, and unleashed the hounds of hell if anyone dared ask him to do any work.

My worst fears came to pass at a business lunch I was late to. The only seat left was next to Raymond and the wall. He sat with his back to me, talking to the person to his right about the merits of compound adjectives (there aren't any).

I munched on bread and stared at the wall before trying to join in the conversation. 'Adjectives are overrated,' I said, which was a pointless statement but I was scraping the bottom of the conversational barrel. Raymond looked at me with his translucent blue eyes, adjusted his wonky red tie, then swivelled around and kept his back to me for the rest of the lunch.

When he was eventually made redundant, he became a freelance journalist, but he was not at all in demand because he was too prickly, tricky and unfriendly. Being liked clearly was not Raymond's mission.

At the other end of the spectrum are those who desperately want to be liked. Most people would prefer to be liked, but it is liberating when you can accept that you won't get on with everyone. A mission to be liked is doomed to failure – there is always someone who will snipe about something you have done or failed to do. Defaulting to people-pleasing mode can backfire if you end up resenting the unfair advantage you have given someone else in a bid to get them to like you.

Remembering names, being positive, showing an interest in others and being reliable will encourage others to warm to you. But going overboard can be damaging, as Sally Field discovered when she accepted the Oscar for Best Actress in 1985. 'I can't deny the fact that you like me,' she said. 'Right now, you like me!' After that speech, many did not.

What do the Stoics say?

Gladiatorial games were very popular across all classes throughout the Roman Empire. However, Marcus Aurelius resisted the urge to feed their popularity because he was opposed to bloodshed and forbade sharp weapons on bouts he witnessed. He disliked these games to the point of ignoring the crowds, preferring to read and work. This earned him a ticking-off from his teacher, Fronto, who was concerned it would make him unpopular.

Marcus believed it was a waste of time to worry about other people's opinions. And yet it is difficult not to be conscious of what others think.

Everyone wants to be liked, but can someone's opinion of us determine how likeable we are? Mastering the art of separating fact from opinion helps bring perspective to concerns about what others think. Attaching self-worth to the opinions of others fuels worry. Letting their opinions wash over you, having discarded the need to be liked, frees you from the shackles.

A FINAL WORD FROM MARCUS AURELIUS

'But perhaps the desire of the thing called fame
will torment you. See how soon everything is
forgotten, and look at the chaos of infinite time
on each side of the present, and the emptiness
of applause, and the changeableness and want of
judgement in those who pretend to give praise,
and the narrowness of the space within which it
is circumscribed, and be quiet at last.'
Meditations, 4.3

RULE 46

BRING YOURSELF TO WORK, BUT NOT YOUR WHOLE SELF

It is Monday, and someone asks what you did on the weekend. Do you say you did several loads of washing, argued with your partner about the dishwasher and then wondered whether you should have become an astronaut and lived on the International Space Station?

'Bringing your whole self to work' is a concept that attempts to unite our work self with our non-work self. It is well-intentioned, based on the idea that revealing our whole selves to our workmates will promote greater understanding, and therefore more effective ways of collaborating. But there are things you say at work, and things you do not say. Even though we spend more time with our work colleagues than with our partners, the level of disclosure at work is determined by an unspoken social code.

All of us have mix of good and questionable attributes. Bringing the whole shebang to work would create problems. Your work self plans ahead, attends meetings and discreetly eats a salad sandwich for lunch. You suggest a deeper analysis on a project to make sure you have covered all the issues. Your home self leaves the bedsheets on for three weeks, ditches a mate's pub night to binge-watch a show and eats ice cream straight from the tub.

The sci-fi series *Severance* takes this concept to an extreme level. Workers at Lumon Industries are implanted with a chip to create an 'innie' self for the workplace and an 'outie' self that takes over once they leave the office. Neither version interacts with the other, which means the organisation can ring-fence its shadowy work.

Similarly, the social code of the real-life workplace is that we only reveal the parts of ourselves that make us more efficient and effective. Steve from partnerships once said to me, 'I really like the way you bring your whole self to work.' But actually it was a dig at my snow dome collection. Despite companies encouraging us to bring our whole self to work, we need to know exactly which bits.

More fundamentally, what does 'bringing your whole self' even mean? Telling Leanne from business development I find her annoying? Not really. Leading workshops on the bird life of Patagonia? Not during work hours. Wearing a Freddy Krueger costume? Not unless it's Halloween.

The 'whole self' philosophy is fraught. In my experience, the only reason work relationships remain intact is because we don't blurt out what's on our mind. If I told Sharon from finance that Donald Trump had a better personality than her, I might soon be out of a job.

The 'whole self' mindset also depends on where you are on the ladder of success. By the time you reach C-suite, you can definitely let your freak flag fly, and bring your family along for the ride, because you no longer need to prove yourself. You've already made it to the top. As for the rest of us mugs on the lower rungs, we just need to show we're good at our job.

What do the Stoics say?

The Stoics believed that the *logos* was the animating force behind the world. At the individual level, this is our human reason. On a cosmic level, it is the rational principle that governs and connects the cosmos and our true natures.

'The mutual dependence all things have . . . is worth your frequent observation . . . for one thing comes in order after another, and this comes through their active movement and harmony, and the unity of their substance,' Marcus Aurelius wrote.

Failing to recognise our true nature and our interconnectedness with others leads to suffering. The *logos* that governs our true nature causes no harm.

'And what principles are those?' Marcus wrote. 'Such as state and distinguish good and evil. Such as give us to understand that there is nothing properly good for a man but what promotes the virtues of justice, temperance, fortitude, and independence, nor anything bad for him, but that which carries him off to the contrary vices.'

As a Stoic, bringing your whole self to work would be no trouble, because your behaviour would be in accordance with nature. Stoics describe this as the inner manifestation of universal reason that cushions the swell of emotion, such as your frustration when you're on the phone to IT for three hours.

If you become a Stoic sage – that is, a person who always invokes the Stoic virtues – then bringing your whole self to work carries no risk, either. There's no chance you'll blurt out how boring Gary from IT is, because you will have impeccable self-control. But sagely behaviour is more something to aspire to than ever realistically attain, given our behavioural limitations. Making progress towards this ideal is all that matters.

A FINAL WORD FROM MARCUS AURELIUS

'Be contented you have a governing intelligence within you, and if the waves run too high, let them carry away your body, your breath, and all things else, but there is no necessity your mind should be driven with them.'
Meditations, 12.14

RULE 46. BRING YOURSELF TO WORK, BUT NOT YOUR WHOLE SELF

RULE 47

MANAGE YOUR EGO

A company decided to expand its audience by publishing a summary of its quarterly updates, which had ballooned to 10,000 words. The goal was to engage the kind of audience who don't like dense blocks of text. So they decided to issue the update in a simple format for everyday, time-poor people.

A meeting was arranged with the author, Gerard, who felt he was not only good with numbers but with words. He sprinkled his financial updates with terms like 'vis-à-vis', 'aforementioned' and 'multifarious', which resonated with almost no one. Yet he luxuriated in the belief that his linguistic panache meant he should continue publishing a quarterly thesis that drove away audiences.

The team responsible for deconstructing his impenetrable prose held a pre-meeting meeting to discuss how to delicately tell someone with a towering ego that his work needed editing. Veronique, who worked in communications, took the lead. 'Let me handle this,' she began. 'I'll tell him that we will not under any circumstances back down, regardless of what he says.'

When the team met with Gerard, Veronique pitched the idea: they would summarise his work in an effort to bring it to a wider audience. 'More people will appreciate your excellent insights,' she said.

The author nodded solemnly and leant back, hands behind his head. 'I am violently opposed to this idea,' he said.

With that, the project was shut down and his verbose updates continued to engage almost no one.

Our ego manages the onslaught of external information we receive every day, filtering it through our thoughts, emotions, opinions, ideologies and belief systems. But it can also bring out the worst in us, encouraging us to blame others, to ignore feedback or to avoid responsibility, usually for fear of failure. You don't even need to be self-absorbed to be tripped up by ego.

In his book *Ego Is the Enemy*, American author Ryan Holiday cautions against being seduced by the stories we tell ourselves about how amazing we are. He encourages us to surround ourselves with friends who can keep our ego in check. Such friends can help us make changes, take risks and discard our concerns about the past and the future.

What do the Stoics say?

Egos expect recognition, compensation and plenty of compliments for their achievements, and are crushed when their efforts are met with indifference. A big ego places us at the centre of our own world, distorting our perception by elevating our importance. It can be an impediment to progress, because it overestimates our abilities.

When Alexander the Great met the Cynic philosopher Diogenes, who was enjoying a spot of sunbathing, Alexander asked how he could help. Diogenes was not wealthy and could have asked for anything, but instead he requested that Alexander 'stop blocking my sun'. In that moment, Diogenes took a scythe to Alexander's ego.

Humility is the antidote to an unrestrained ego. It helps us accept that we have limited control over rewards, recognition and validation that come from other people. Being less invested in outcomes switches the focus to what you can control – and that is doing your work to the best of your ability, regardless of how things turn out.

Marcus Aurelius advises that we focus on our own rather than other people's actions, and cautions against measuring our self-worth by the trappings of the external world. This means resisting the ego's powerful desire for praise and recognition. And ignoring the likes of Gerard.

'He who loves fame considers another man's activity to be his own good,' Marcus Aurelius reminded himself, 'and he who loves pleasure, his own sensations; but he who has understanding, considers his own acts to be his own good.'

The Roman Senate offered Marcus military titles – Armeniacus and Parthicus – for his armies' victories over the Armenians and the Parthians. He initially refused them, but eventually accepted both, although he had played no field role in either war. So perhaps even Marcus was not entirely indifferent to recognition.

A FINAL WORD FROM MARCUS AURELIUS

'What then is it that you count worth your esteem? Applause? Not at all. Why, then, you must not value the applause of tongues, for the commendation of the multitude is nothing else … What, then, is there behind worth the having? To govern your motions, and make use of your being according to the intentions of nature.'
Meditations, 6.16

RULE 48

RESIGN WELL

When your workload spirals out of control, Steve from partnerships delivers another withering putdown in a meeting and your boss contacts you at 10 pm for an update on a project, sometimes the best thing to do is to ditch the job altogether.

In recent times we have emerged from our pandemic-affected working life with broader horizons, changed perspectives and less tolerance for office shenanigans. This has prompted many people to embrace some large-scale life changes, including new jobs.

Of course, sometimes the decision to leave is foisted upon a worker by their employer. This can be done either overtly, or through a phenomenon known as 'quiet firing', which means sidelining underperforming employees. This is the antithesis of 'quiet quitting', whereby workers do the bare minimum to get by without actually leaving their job. Quiet firing relegates an employee to a diminished role, in they hope they'll get fed up and resign.

Knowing when to quit is a skill. If you reach breaking point because Leanne from business development speaks in an adenoidal voice, then it might be worth you thinking about a bigger change – maybe you're not cut out for this type of work. If your boss fails to understand basic work boundaries and drowns you in work until you reach breaking point, then it could be time to go.

I learnt the art of quitting at the age of ten during a school swimming carnival. I was trailing the 50-metre race by half a lap. The others had finished and the crowd slow-clapped me as I struggled on for another ten metres. Eventually the organiser got on his megaphone and told me to get out of the pool because the next race was starting. The experience taught me a valuable lesson: the expectation that we should persevere and finish no matter what is misguided.

Why stick at a job that brings you no joy if you have the option of finding employment elsewhere? There are cognitive forces that discourage us from quitting and push us to continue sinking our emotional energy, time and effort into something that isn't right. We are hardwired to stick with the status quo.

The pandemic and a tight job market have left many of us contemplating our places in the work universe. A friend who works as a school counsellor said: 'Another of my colleagues just resigned, so our team of five is now down to me and a girl half my age who has never heard of Chevy Chase. Am thinking I might not go back!'

After a bad day, it is easy to indulge the resignation fantasy. Do you leave a copy of *How to Manage Difficult People* on your manager's desk? Or do you do you stand up at your workstation and say, 'See you later, suckers!' before kicking a bin over and messing up Steve's hair on your way out? Maybe you simply ghost the place, and just don't turn up the next day? Or you could adopt Richard Nixon's approach with a one-sentence resignation letter: 'I hereby resign the Office of the President of the United States.' If you are looking for even more brevity, you could just text your boss one word: 'Enough.'

The trouble with bridge burning is that you will probably need a new job, and you might well need a good reference to get it. You never know when you might need something from that annoying boss in the future. So unless you have suddenly inherited a vast sum of money, you really have no option but to make a dignified exit.

Resigning well takes courage. It's a less seismic version of ending a relationship. And it's not just about communicating your decision to go in a respectful way. Working during your notice period can feel like swimming in glue. The effort required to do the job magnifies because all incentive has gone. Yet this is the period that your colleagues will remember most. Goofing off at work, disappearing for three-hour lunches and simply not doing any work will become your legacy. Best to do the hard yards for a few weeks and leave on a high note.

Most important of all, resist the urge to deliver any unflattering feedback on your way out. Any comfort it might provide when you say to your boss that it's them and not you that caused you to leave may be only temporary: when you analyse your job history, you may spot a pattern of getting annoyed and leaving countless jobs. In the end, it probably is just you and not them.

When you decide to leave, it's best to do so swiftly instead of lingering over the decision and expending too much mental energy over it (see Rule 23). You don't need to wait around for evidence that it's the right decision or get permission from anyone. You just need to know you want to go.

On the upside, after you leave, you suddenly realise the workplace that dominated your working hours is not, in fact, the centre of the universe, as you had assumed. It's just another company vying for attention in an already crowded marketplace. And you think of all the hours spent you spent agonising over the people, the meetings, the workload and the stuff-ups that kept you awake at 3 am and wonder, 'What was all that about?'

What do the Stoics say?

Marcus Aurelius did not get the opportunity to resign from his job as emperor, but when he knew his end was near – likely by plague – he reportedly said, 'Why do you weep for me, rather not think of the plague and death that is common to all?'

Marcus would advise quitting with virtue and not succumbing to the temptation of telling your boss what you really think. He looked to others as role models of virtuous behaviour.

'Nothing delights so much as the examples of the virtues, when they are exhibited in the morals of those who live with us and present themselves in abundance, as far as is possible. We must keep them before us.'

The narrative we construct about our experience at work might be at odds with reality, of course. Or maybe our work gripes are justified. 'Do not trouble yourself about other people's faults, but leave them with those that must answer for them,' Marcus said.

When confronted with life's big challenges, the Stoics reminded themselves of their own mortality. Resignation is about endings. A death of a phase of life before another begins. The Latin phrase *memento mori* – which means 'remember you will die' or 'remember that you are mortal' – encapsulates how the Stoics created perspective and a sense of urgency in their lives.

In *Meditations*, Marcus wrote about not waiting to live a life of virtue. 'Manage all your actions, words and thoughts accordingly,' he pointed out, 'since you may at any moment quit life.' His own life was often imperilled – by plagues, invading armies, assassins and poor health – and he endured the deaths of many friends, colleagues and family members. This was all the more reason, he argued, to keep life in perspective by considering the prospect of death.

Seneca also meditated on death in order to live better. 'Let us prepare our minds as if we'd come to the very end of life,' he wrote. 'Let us postpone nothing. Let us balance life's books each day . . . The one who puts the finishing touches on their life each day is never short of time.'

A FINAL WORD FROM MARCUS AURELIUS

'The spherical form of the soul maintains its figure, when it is neither extended towards any object, nor contracted inwards, nor dispersed nor sinks down, but is illuminated by light, by which it sees the truth, the truth of all things and the truth that is in itself.'

Meditations, 11.12

RULE 49

WIN LOTTO

If your job fails to spark any inspiration and the people at work get your goat, the obvious solution is to win Lotto. Then you can tell your boss that there are microbes on Mars with more talent than him.

The odds of winning the jackpot range somewhere in the order of 1 in 45,379,620 for OzLotto in Australia, 1 in 140,000,000 for the EuroMillions, and a discouraging 1 in 292,201,338 for Powerball. The best odds are the Irish Lotto at 1 in 10,737,573.

Is lottery thinking really the way to go? After all, a UQ mathematician, Professor Peter Adams, calculated that Australians have a 1 in 12,000 chance of being struck by lightning. Even better are the odds that someone will be killed by space junk this decade: just one in ten. This mindset might actually prevent you from doing the hard work to get what you want.

There are things you can do to increase your chance of a Lotto windfall. You could choose a lottery with better odds, you could join a syndicate or you could choose 'lucky' numbers. Another way of increasing your odds is to play more often, according to Lottoland (which wants you to play more).

If you happen to strike it lucky and land a first-division win, do you continue working, throw in the towel but work through your notice period, or disappear without a trace, leaving a half-drunk mug of coffee on your desk and a picture of your dog Barney?

When the pandemic kicked off, I got news that a friend had won a multi-million-dollar house, a car and bars of gold in a lottery. This sent those of us working increasingly longer hours with no reprieve spiralling into bleakness, as we contemplated the injustice of the universe. Really, we should have been happy, because her win showed that lotteries are not total scams. But they are also very unlikely.

The sad fact is that the best odds you have of finding happiness and success are to work hard and cultivate a side hustle that, if it goes well, might allow you to break the shackles of being a salaried employee. As those of us who've lined up with the other mugs and splurged our money on the lottery know all too well, of course, flights of fancy are a road to misery when your numbers never come up.

What do the Stoics say?

Marcus Aurelius effectively won the Lotto when at age 18 he was adopted by the imperial heir Antoninus Pius. And while Marcus's family was wealthy and he had a job for life, he could not escape the pitfalls of his job.

Ultimately, he believed that we make our own good fortune. And that luck alone is too fickle to rely on, because it can change on a dime. One minute you're on top of your game, and the next you're swimming in a sea of confusion and despondency. And then things turn around.

If our happiness is tied to things beyond our control, then the unexpected swings of fortune in life powerfully influence our thoughts and reactions. Our wealth or status, other people's opinions, our looks and the weather forecast can't be changed easily. Being indifferent to anything dictated by fortune, whether for good or bad, builds greater resilience in us for when the tide turns.

The more independent – even indifferent – to these things you can make your life, the more secure your position will be. The less subject you will be to that cruel, fickle mistress that is Fortune.

Seneca had a lot to say about Fortune: 'harsh and invincible is her power; things deserved and undeserved must we suffer just as she wills . . . Like a mistress that is changeable and passionate and neglectful of her slaves, she will be capricious in both her rewards and her punishments. What need is there to weep over parts of life? The whole of it calls for tears.'

Striking good fortune falls squarely outside our sphere of control. But it is worth remembering that being born in the first place is the greatest good fortune of all. Experiencing the disappointment of not winning wads of cash puts you ahead of the bazillion people who were never born. They will never know what it's like spending eons in meetings that stretch to infinity and conversing with work zombies day in, day out. But with a little Stoic guidance, it is possible to not only be grateful for being alive but actually make your job more tolerable – on a good day, meaningful, even? – and bring some enlightenment to your work universe.

A FINAL WORD FROM MARCUS AURELIUS

'I was once a fortunate man, but I lost it, I know not how. But fortunate means that a man has assigned to himself a good fortune: and a good fortune is good disposition of the soul, good emotions, good actions.'
Meditations, 5.36

RULE 49. WIN LOTTO

NOTES

Among the many editions of Marcus Aurelius's *Meditations* are the following, on which I have relied for translations:

Jeremy Collier, *The Meditations of Marcus Aurelius* (George Routledge & Sons, London, 1894)

Gregory Hays, *Meditations* (The Modern Library, New York, 2002)

C. Scot Hicks & David V. Hicks, *The Emperor's Handbook: A New Translation of The Meditations* (Simon & Schuster, New York, 2002)

Francis Hutcheson & James Moor, *The Meditations of the Emperor Marcus Aurelius Antoninus* (Liberty Fund, Carmel, IN, 2008)

George Long, *The Thoughts of the Emperor Marcus Aurelius Antoninus* (Little, Brown and Company, Boston, 1889)

Epigraph

'At dawn, when you have trouble . . .': *Meditations*, 5.1 (Hays).

Introduction

'You have passed through life . . .': Seneca, *Letters from a Stoic*.

'Do not suppose you are hurt . . .': *Meditations*, 4.7 (Collier).

'The impediment to action . . .': *Meditations*, 5.20 (Hays).

'Be not heavy in business . . .': *Meditations*, 8.51 (Collier).

Rule 1

'the consiglieri of the corporate world . . .': 'Where next for management's consiglieri?', *The Economist*, 4 October 2022.

'One must be thoroughly informed . . .': *Meditations*, 11.18 (Collier).

'When you are most angry and vexed . . .': *Meditations*, 11.18 (Collier).

'Begin the morning by saying . . .': *Meditations*, 2.1 (Long).

'It is a great folly . . .': *Meditations*, 7.71 (Collier).

'Rational creatures are designed . . .': *Meditations*, 7.55 (Collier).

'If anything external vexes you . . .': *Meditations*, 8.47 (Collier).

Rule 2

'like the promontory against which . . .': *Meditations*, 4.49 (Long).

'Have a care you have not . . .': *Meditations*, 6.30 (Collier).

'The gods live forever . . .': *Meditations*, 7.70 (Hays).

Rule 3

'a far-fetched word . . .': *The Correspondence of Marcus Cornelius Fronto with Marcus Aurelius Antoninus, Lucius Verus, Antoninus Pius, and Various Friends*, vols 1–2, translated and edited by C.R. Haines, Loeb Classical Library (Harvard University Press, Cambridge, MA, 1919).

'Do not dress your thought . . .': *Meditations*, 3.5 (Hicks & Hicks).

Rule 4

'strive to live only what is really your life . . .': *Meditations*, 12.3 (Long).

'Always go by the shortest way to work . . .': *Meditations*, 4.51 (Collier).

Rule 5

'The chief task in life is simply this . . .': Epictetus, *Discourses*, 2.5.4–5.

'One's own mind is a place . . .': *Meditations*, 4.3 (Collier).

Rule 6

'consider how many men . . .': *Meditations*, 4.3 (Collier).

'Your intellect is not affected . . .': *Meditations*, 4.3 (Collier).

'You have it in your power . . .': *Meditations*, 6.52 (Hutcheson & Moor).

Rule 7

'most likely to act with competence . . .': C. Northcote Parkinson, *The Law* (John Murray, New York, 1979), p. 185.

'We are made for cooperation . . .': *Meditations*, 2.1 (Long).

Rule 8

'How unfortunate has this accident made me . . .': *Meditations*, 4.49 (Collier).

'Here you must remember to proportion . . .': *Meditations*, 4.32 (Collier).

'Your manners will depend very much . . .': *Meditations*, 5.16 (Collier).

'All things are opinion . . .': *Meditations*, 12.22 (Collier).

'If this accident is no fault of mine . . .': *Meditations*, 5.35 (Collier).

Rule 9

'It is just that you should suffer . . .': *Meditations*, 8.22a (Hutcheson & Moor).

'everything harmonises with me . . .': *Meditations*, 4.23 (Long).

'Remember how often you have postponed . . .': *Meditations*, 2.4 (Collier).

Rule 10

'you can . . . commit injustice by doing nothing': *Meditations*, 9.5 (Hays).

'And yet former British prime minister . . .': Neel Burton, 'Laziness can be productive. You just need to put some work into it', *Scroll.in*, 19 October 2019.

'consume whole days . . .': Dio Cassius, *Roman History*, vol. IX, book 72.

'It is essential that we . . .': Epictetus, *Discourses*.

'In one way an arrow moves . . .': *Meditations*, 8.60 (Long).

Rule 11

'perform every action as though . . .': *Meditations*, 2.5 (Collier).

'Putting things off . . .': Seneca, *On the Shortness of Life*.

'life is long enough . . .': Seneca, *On the Shortness of Life*.

'Do what nature now requires . . .': *Meditations*, 9.29 (Long).

Rule 12

'I have often wondered . . .': *Meditations*, 12.4 (Collier).

'The power of living well . . .': *Meditations*, 11.16 (Hutcheson & Moor).

Rule 13

'See how soon everything is forgotten . . .': *Meditations*, 4.3 (Long).

'What is praise except . . .': *Meditations*, 4.19 (Long).

'Gaius Caesar, while engaged in . . .': *The Correspondence of Marcus Cornelius Fronto with Marcus Aurelius Antoninus, Lucius Verus, Antoninus Pius, and Various Friends*, vol. 2, translated and edited by C.R. Haines, Loeb Classical Library (Harvard University Press, Cambridge, MA, 1920).

'And here you must guard against flattery . . .': *Meditations*, 11.18 (Collier).

'Short-lived are both the praiser and the praised . . .': *Meditations*, 8.21 (Long).

'Everything which is in any way beautiful . . .': *Meditations*, 4.20 (Long).

'People generally despise where they flatter . . .': *Meditations*, 11.14 (Collier).

Rule 14

'These two maxims be always ready . . .': *Meditations*, 4.3 (Collier).

Rule 15

'We must take a higher view . . .': Seneca, *Of Peace of Mind*, XV.

'I have to die . . .': Epictetus, *Discourses and Selected Writing*, translated and edited by Robert Dobbin (Penguin, London, 2008), 1.32.

'And as for that body that does not transmit light . . .': *Meditations*, 8.57 (Collier).

Rule 16

'Guide your life towards . . .': *Meditations*, 8.32 (Collier).

'For the last two days . . .': *The Correspondence of Marcus Cornelius Fronto with Marcus Aurelius Antoninus, Lucius Verus, Antoninus Pius, and Various Friends*, vol. 2, translated and edited by C.R. Haines, Loeb Classical Library (Harvard University Press, Cambridge, MA, 1920).

'Do everything as a disciple of Antoninus . . .': *Meditations*, 6.30 (Collier).

'Look upon the plants and birds . . .': *Meditations*, 5.1 (Collier).

'Persevere then . . .': *Meditations*, 10.31 (Long).

Rule 17

'If it is not right . . .': *Meditations*, 12.17 (Long).

'We are all cooperating . . .': *Meditations*, 6.42 (Hutcheson & Moor).

'Let no person hear you . . .': *Meditations*, 8.9 (Long).

Rule 18

'You shall sooner see . . .': *Meditations*, 9.9 (Collier).

'Here you must remember . . .': *Meditations*, 4.32 (Collier).

Rule 19

'It is the privilege of human nature . . .': *Meditations*, 7.22 (Collier).

'When you are troubled about anything . . .': *Meditations*, 12.26 (Long).

Rule 20

'Now, what significancy and excellence . . .': *Meditations*, 5.12 (Collier).

'If you should throw dirt or clay at a spring . . .': *Meditations*, 8.51 (Collier).

'Philosophy will put upon you . . .': *Meditations*, 5.9 (Collier).

'Tell me what you meet with . . .': *Meditations*, 8.24 (Collier).

Rule 21

'Monimus, the Cynic philosopher . . .': *Meditations*, 2.15 (Collier).

Rule 22

'the busybody, the ungrateful . . .': *Meditations*, 2.1 (Long).

'Neither can I be angry with my brother . . .': *Meditations*, 2.1 (Hammond).

'If an antagonist in the circus . . .': *Meditations*, 6.20 (Collier).

Rule 23

'A *Review of Economics Studies* paper . . .': Steven D. Levitt, 'Heads or tails: The impact of a coin toss on major life decisions and subsequent happiness', *Review of Economic Studies*, vol. 88, no. 1, 2021, pp. 378–405.

'If the gods . . . will take care of none of us . . .': *Meditations*, 6.44 (Collier).

Rule 24

'Together, we create the extraordinary': Aaron Patrick, 'Ashurst should accept its purpose is not extraordinary', *Australian Financial Review*, 22 July 2022.

'Nothing is so likely to raise the mind . . .': *Meditations*, 3.11 (Collier).

'Do external things distract you? . . .': *Meditations*, 2.7 (Hays).

Rule 25

'to live with desire . . .': Epictetus, *Discourses*, Chapter XII.

'But he that runs riot out of desire . . .': *Meditations*, 2.10 (Collier).

Rule 26

'Where things appear most plausible . . .': *Meditations*, 6.13 (Collier).

'He that can overlook his body . . .': *Meditations*, 12.2 (Collier).
Rule 27
'How much better it is . . .': Seneca, *Letters from a Stoic*, 83.17.
'There is no living without rest . . .': *Meditations*, 5.1 (Collier).
Rule 28
'Wash yourself clean . . .': *Meditations*, 7.31 (Hays).
Rule 29
'Not every one's good opinion . . .': *Meditations*, 3.4 (Collier).
Rule 30
'Sometimes even to live is an act of courage': Seneca, *Moral Letters to Lucilius*.
'Virtue alone affords everlasting . . .': Seneca, *Moral Letters to Lucilius*, 27.
'I judge you unfortunate . . .': Seneca, *On Providence*.
'No tree becomes rooted . . .': Seneca, *On Providence*.
'To be vexed at anything . . .': *Meditations*, 2.16 (Collier).
Rule 31
'British former *Financial Times* columnist . . .': Lucy Kellaway, 'How I lost my 25-year battle against corporate claptrap', *Financial Times*, 16 July 2017.
'Has any advantage happened to you? . . .': *Meditations*, 4.26 (Collier).
'Motions and changes are continually . . .': *Meditations*, 6.15 (Long).
'The world subsists upon change . . .': *Meditations*, 4.2 (Collier).
Rule 32
'Nikola Tesla had an insight . . .': Emma Seppälä, 'Happiness research shows the biggest obstacle to creativity is being too busy', *Quartz*, 8 May 2017.
'The art of life . . .': *Meditations*, 7.61 (Long).
'But those who love their several arts . . .': *Meditations*, 5.1 (Long).
Rule 33
'you may free yourself . . .': *Meditations*, 9.32 (Collier).
'Continually study the history of nature . . .': *Meditations*, 10.11 (Collier).
'Look round at the courses of the stars . . .': *Meditations*, 7.47 (Long).
Rule 34
'The British writer Oliver Burkeman . . .': *Four Thousand Weeks: Time Management for Mortals* (Penguin, New York, 2021).
'We're tight-fisted with property and money . . .': Seneca, *On the Shortness of Life*.
'snatches away each day as it comes . . .': Seneca, *On the Shortness of Life*.
'Time is like a river . . .': *Meditations*, 4.43 (Long).

Rule 35

'For the greater part of what we say and do . . .': *Meditations*, 4.24 (Collier).

'Be sure you entertain no fancies . . .': *Meditations*, 2.5 (Collier).

'You see what a few points . . .': *Meditations*, 2.5 (Collier).

Rule 36

'For as the universal nature . . .': *Meditations*, 8.35 (Collier).

'He is a madman . . .': *Meditations*, 11.33 (Collier).

'Leave these unnatural changes . . .': *Meditations*, 7.58 (Hutcheson & Moor).

Rule 37

'The reason we have two ears . . .': Diogenes Laertius, *Lives of Eminent Philosophers*.

'Accustom yourself to attend carefully . . .': *Meditations*, 6.53 (Long).

'Do not let either discourse or action . . .': *Meditations*, 7.4 (Collier).

Rule 38

'It is inevitable if you enter . . .': Epictetus, *Discourses*.

'The best revenge . . .': *Meditations*, 6.6 (Hays).

Rule 39

'As you are a member of society yourself . . .': *Meditations*, 9.23 (Collier).

'That which is not good for the swarm . . .': *Meditations*, 6.54 (Long).

'Our fellowship is very similar . . .': Seneca, *Epistles*, 95.53.

'Men exist for the sake . . .': *Meditations*, 8.59 (Long).

Rule 40

'When any accident happens . . .': *Meditations*, 7.58 (Collier).

'And this was not God's will . . .': *Meditations*, 8.56 (Long).

Rule 41

'It is impossible for a person . . .': Epictetus, *Discourses*.

'Nothing is more scandalous . . .': *Meditations*, 12.27 (Collier).

'A fleet horse or greyhound . . .': *Meditations*, 5.6 (Collier).

'Remind yourself that your task . . .': *Meditations*, 8.5 (Hays).

'Receive wealth or prosperity . . .': *Meditations*, 8.33 (Long).

Rule 42

'Fruitlessly searching for lost items . . .': Libby Sander, 'The case for finally cleaning your desk', *Harvard Business Review*, 25 March 2019.

'One needs no silver plate . . .': Seneca, *On the Shortness of Life*.

'Wealth consists not in having great possessions . . .': Epictetus, *Discourses*.

'The greater part of your trouble . . .': *Meditations*, 9.32 (Collier).

Rule 43

'Australian columnist and author Jane Caro . . .': 'Why happiness lies somewhere between boredom and fear', *Sydney Morning Herald*, 19 December 2021.

'manage what lies before you . . .': *Meditations*, 3.12 (Collier).

'In a word, happiness lies all . . .': *Meditations*, 5.36 (Collier).

Rule 44

'Remember that you ought to behave . . .': Epictetus, *Discourses*.

'When the hearing and smelling . . .': *Meditations*, 10.35 (Collier).

Rule 45

'But perhaps the desire . . .': *Meditations*, 4.3 (Long).

Rule 46

'The mutual dependence all things have . . .': *Meditations*, 6.38 (Collier).

'And what principles are those? . . .': *Meditations*, 8.1 (Collier).

'Be you contented . . .': *Meditations*, 12.14 (Collier).

Rule 47

'Ryan Holiday cautions . . .': *Ego Is the Enemy* (Profile Books, London, 2016).

'He who loves fame . . .': *Meditations*, 6.51 (Long).

'What then is it . . .': *Meditations*, 6.16 (Collier).

Rule 48

'Why do you weep for me . . .': *Lives of the Later Caesars*, translated and edited by A. Birley (Penguin Books, London, 1976), p. 136.

'Nothing delights so much as . . .': *Meditations*, 6.48 (Long).

'Do not trouble yourself . . .': *Meditations*, 7.29 (Collier).

'Manage all your actions . . .': *Meditations*, 2.11 (Collier).

'Let us prepare our minds . . .': Seneca, *Moral Letters to Lucilius*, 101.

'The spherical form of the soul . . .': *Meditations*, 11.12 (Long).

Rule 49

'harsh and invincible is her power . . .': Seneca, *Of Consolation*, XI.

'I was once a fortunate man . . .': *Meditations*, 5.36 (Long).

ACKNOWLEDGEMENTS

First up, I'd like to thank the makers of peanut M&Ms, Wagon Wheels and Moro bars for sustaining me during late-night and early-morning writing sessions while I was also juggling a full-time job, teenagers, two kittens and a family of snails that moved in (see Rule 9).

Thank you to my primary source researcher, Anthony Congedo, who stepped outside his Roman history comfort zone of 250–40 BCE to draw some creative threads between the wisdom of Marcus Aurelius and eating pretzels on the loo at work. His meticulous research provided credibility and balance to the absurdity, and unearthed some fascinating historical insights. Thank you also for always keeping the house afloat, and the kids and cats fed, watered and doted on.

This book would have remained a figment of my imagination without Jane Willson from Murdoch Books, whose talent I just assume comes from some metaphysical realm. She took a punt after a long conversation about the quirks of email sign-offs, and helped transform a few lines of an introduction into a book that (hopefully) amuses and informs readers in need of Stoic inspiration in the workplace.

My sincere gratitude also to editorial manager Justin Wolfers for his proficient and professional guidance, with a welcomed side dollop of sunniness. His vision, skill and experience are greatly appreciated. And to Julian Welch, an accomplished editor whose talent, warmth and insights smoothed the rougher edges of the manuscript and drew a coherent line between *Meditations* and some very offbeat subjects. His patience and endurance during the intense referencing phase were indeed Stoical.

I'm deeply grateful for the towering talent of Oslo Davis, whose brilliant cartoons made me laugh out loud. His contribution brought to life some bizarre topics in a way that made me want to recreate his imagery at work. Thank you to Kristy Allen and Jo Thomson for their superb book and cover design, which I both love and find very funny. They were unwavering despite the endless demands for tweaks.

My sincere gratitude to the Triangle of Tremendousness, a group comprising me and two colleagues who made me laugh every day at a previous workplace, despite the high pressure, horrendous deadlines and hygiene lapses from some of our co-workers (see Rules 20 and 28). They inspired this book, and I will continue to lobby them to take our office banter into the podcast world.

Thank you also to Dunstan Power, whose friendship, support and editing suggestions helped sharpen the anecdotes and spur me on during ungodly hours thanks to our time-zone difference. Dunstan embodies Stoic virtue and showed me the juggle was possible after he churned out his mountaineering thriller, *The Empty Rope*, while running his company, playing drums in a band and being a sensational parent to his kids.

Thank you also to my journo mates, the Velvet Booth Goals, Laurie chicks and other friends, family and former colleagues (and foes), for sharing their stories of the ups and downs of working life. Thank you to the lovely Kate Arnott for her audio-visual support, and Catherine Chisholm for leading me astray in my journalism career and creating such good book fodder. You're both top chicks.

Thank you to Sam and Serena Lawson, my siblings, whom I feel compelled to mention so the next family catch-up isn't awkward. And also to feline siblings Yoshi and Boo, two balls of fluffy cuteness who are the best work colleagues of all, mainly because they can't speak.

Finally, a big, warm thank you to Henry and Finny, for tolerating their mother's parenting and domestic neglect over several months while I was in the throes of writing madness. They always keep me grounded, especially when I ask if they will ever read this book and they respond with: 'Depends on how long it takes.'

Published in 2023 by Murdoch Books, an imprint of Allen & Unwin
Text copyright © Annie Lawson 2023

Murdoch Books Australia
Cammeraygal Country
83 Alexander Street,
Crows Nest NSW 2065
Phone: +61 (0)2 8425 0100
murdochbooks.com.au
info@murdochbooks.com.au

Murdoch Books UK
Ormond House,
26–27 Boswell Street,
London WC1N 3JZ
Phone: +44 (0) 20 8785 5995
murdochbooks.co.uk
info@murdochbooks.co.uk

A catalogue record for this
book is available from the
National Library of Australia

A catalogue record for this book is available from the British Library

ISBN 978 1 92261 673 9

Cover design by Jo Thomson
Illustrations by Oslo Davis
Text design by Kristy Allen / Jo Thomson

Typeset by Midland Typesetters
Printed and bound C&C Offset
Printing Co. Ltd., China

We acknowledge that we meet and work on the traditional lands of the Cammeraygal
people of the Eora Nation and pay our respects to their elders past, present and future.

10 9 8 7 6 5 4 3 2 1

MIX
Paper | Supporting
responsible forestry
FSC® C008047